PRAISE FOR F[...]

'A 21st-century Lewis Carroll. The best quizmasters aim to delight, and *Cryptic Pub Quiz* does so on every page. This is quizzing where you know the answer but find it only after delicious mental contortions. Relentlessly creative, frequently hilarious and consistently beautiful'

Alan Connor, author of *The Joy of Quiz*
and question editor for *Richard Osman's House Of Games*

'I am most impressed... the questions should offer an enjoyable challenge to those adept at cryptic crossword solving'

Tim Moorey, author of *How to Crack Cryptic Crosswords*

'Frank Paul is an extremely impressive chap and a dazzling quizzer; I will be very excited to see his quiz book'

Victoria Coren Mitchell, presenter of *Only Connect*

'Frank Paul's quizzes are learning dressed up to have fun – aerobics of the mind, push-ups of the brain, and tickles of the funny bone.'

Richard Lederer, author of *Anguished English*
and *Get Thee to a Punnery*
and former co-host of *A Way with Words*

'Dull men in pubs across the country, who downloaded their quiz for £5 that morning, will ask you the capital of Peru, or who presented *The Generation Game* after Bruce Forsyth. They are not worthy to lick Frank Paul's boots.'

Marcus Berkmann, *Daily Mail*

THE CRYPTIC
PUB QUIZ

FRANK PAUL

ONEWORLD

A Oneworld Book

This edition published by Oneworld in 2024
First published by Duckworth Overlook in 2017

Text and illustrations © Frank Paul, 2017, 2024

ISBN 978-0-86154-399-1
eISBN 978-0-86154-398-4

Typeset by Danny Lyle
Printed and bound in Great Britain by Clays Ltd, Elcograf S.p.A.

Oneworld Publications
10 Bloomsbury Street
London WC1B 3SR
England

Stay up to date with the latest books,
special offers, and exclusive content from
Oneworld with our newsletter

Sign up on our website
oneworld-publications.com

MIX
Paper | Supporting
responsible forestry
FSC® C018072

This book is dedicated to my gran, my mum, Masha, Eve, Lawrie and Daphna, who have always offered their immense love and support, and also to Andrew Begg and Tom Short, two school friends to whom, as a teenager, I made separate promises that if ever I had a book published I would dedicate it to them.

CONTENTS

PART THREE:
MAKING CONNECTIONS

PART FOUR:
POETIC JUSTICE

PART FIVE:
WORDPLAY

PART SIX:
LET'S GO EXPLORING

PREFACE

SELF-PORTRAIT WALKING ACROSS MIDSUMMER COMMON ON THE WAY TO THE PUB

I have always loved puzzles. As a child, I would draw mazes, making them as complicated as I could, filling the page with tiny paths, eager to watch my mum meander through them with her finger. She was the one I trusted most to solve my mazes, as only she had worked out my secret, never-spoken rule: that I would only be satisfied if she blundered down every single dead end before reaching the exit. I later fell under the spell of a book by one Norman D. Willis, whom I pictured as suave and heroic. His puzzles were set in enthrallingly bizarre worlds populated by people who only lied or only told the truth or alternated between truth and lies. I created my own versions, which I would spring on my mum. The more I worked on these puzzles, the more elaborate they became, until she could no longer figure them out. After gazing at the puzzle with a slightly tragic air, punctuated by marvelling at my ingenuity – as if *that* in itself would placate me – she would entreat me to let her give up. I urged her to persevere, to give me the pleasure of witnessing her weave together my delicately placed clues, and she would stare with a pained expression for a little longer before declaring that she was stumped. There was no one else I would have felt comfortable showing these puzzles to; if my work had been scoffed at, I would have been crushed.

I had never particularly gone in for quizzes before meeting Masha, the person I would go on to marry. But I grew fonder of them as time went on. We discovered that we enjoyed quizzes for different reasons. She liked the social aspect of quizzing, exchanging suggestions with our friends, discovering more about their experience and interests, feeling a sense of camaraderie strengthened by sharing a common goal. I thrived on the knowledge I could display and the facts that I was acquiring with each new quiz.

When Masha was planning to take up a volunteering placement, the charity asked all of their prospective volunteers to raise funds for them, and among their suggestions was to run a quiz. I'd had idle daydreams about running a quiz before but never considered it in earnest – yet as soon as I heard the suggestion, I was filled with the unshakeable conviction that *this was what I longed to do.*

My debut quiz as a presenter was far from a roaring success. I realised as I read out the questions that it was far too hard, showing no mercy to contestants ignorant of certain fairly obscure pieces of trivia, and I felt the jollity in the atmosphere being palpably sucked from the air. As I'd been compiling the questions, Masha had objected to their difficulty, but I'd assured her that people wouldn't mind because they'd be so looking forward to the interesting facts I would reveal as I announced the answers. She'd been right all along! I wondered what I would change if I ever got the chance to present a quiz again.

My chance came two years later: we heard that the quizmaster at a local pub, The Mill, had retired, and I took over. This time, I made sure to write questions where the answers could be figured out even if the contestants didn't know them at first, questions whose solutions could be deduced – in gratifying penny-dropping moments – from elaborate wordplay or hidden connections. I would be overwhelmed with nerves as I walked from my house to the pub. I would arrive half an hour early, and spend the time pacing the path by the river, dreading the inevitable moment when I would be compelled to start the quiz.

In my first season at The Mill, a girl turned up soon before the quiz was due to start. She asked if I set the quiz. Then she asked what my favourite quiz show was. She posed this second question with a suspicious air which, though tongue-in-cheek, gave the impression that a lot was riding on the answer.

'It's a toss-up between *Pointless* and *Only Connect*,' I replied, apprehensive but taking solace in the fact that I had uttered a sincere opinion which I could defend if necessary. I was unused to being on the receiving end of an interrogation; there was something rather refreshing about it.

'Those are the two *best answers*!' she enthused with wide eyes.

This girl was Lydia; she and her friend Natalie became regulars at the quiz. On Lydia's birthday, the two of them came round for supper. She asked if I'd like to join her and her boyfriend Tom to apply for *Only Connect*. Though applying for *Only Connect* had never occurred to me before (and, she later told me, the idea of asking me to join her in applying had never occurred to her before that instant), I bellowed, 'Yes!' without a moment's hesitation. The show had been a revelation, an inspiration to me, its questions drawn as much from the world of cryptic crosswords as from general knowledge, showing me the glittering path away from straightforward quizzing to something more creative, beautiful and eccentric. The contestants seemed to possess extraordinary reserves of knowledge and powers of deduction.

One warm spring morning, Lydia, Tom and I walked by the dock in Cardiff, asking each other questions from Thomas Eaton's *Guardian* quiz. Our episode of *Only Connect* was to film that day. At the studio – not the gleaming, glass-fronted edifice of my imagination but a long, brown, warehouse-like building nestled in an industrial estate – our opponents' captain regaled us with tales of reaching a record-breaking number of *Fifteen to One* grand finals and winning £14,000 on *Eggheads*. By the time we were called in, my nerves were out of control, my brain like a pinball machine gone haywire. Victoria Coren Mitchell arrived, briskly had a photo taken standing just behind each of the teams, and advised us that we shouldn't worry about getting things wrong because no one at home knew any of the answers. And before I could say 'Stop, I'm not ready!', we were off.

Our opponents built a heart-sinkingly strong lead after Round 1, we clawed our way back on Round 2, and then, on our connecting wall, we were given full marks! But Tom had answered one group of clues with 'Irish presidents' where the correct answer had been 'Taoisigh'; Victoria had let us have the points, but was now deep in conversation with the question-setters via her earpiece. After an agonising, stomach-twisting wait, three points were snatched from our grasp and our opponents had a commanding lead as we entered the final round.

We lost the game by four points. I'd said barely anything over the course of the match, and what I had said had been largely nonsense: I'd persuaded my team to plump for a wrong answer because I'd misheard 'The Steve Miller Band' as 'Steve Miliband', and I'd buzzed in incorrectly on a missing vowels question. I was devastated.

Lydia said after we came out that she must have had bigger disappointments in her life, but she couldn't recall any. We took a train back. Tom was a reassuring presence, confident that we would get to return as one of the two highest-scoring losing teams. He had to change trains early on. For the rest of the journey to Cambridge, Lydia and I tormented ourselves. We brooded on the events of the quiz a thousand times, lamenting everything we should have done differently. I told her I'd wanted to yell, in defiance of all the evidence to the contrary, 'I *am* good at quizzes!' We kept vowing to change the subject, but every time we did, we found that, without even noticing, we'd immediately begun to talk about *Only Connect* again. She told me afterwards that she'd fallen asleep as soon as she got home; I spent an anguished night, only nodding off at six in the morning.

The next eight episodes of the series were being filmed over the following four days: if two losing teams surpassed our score, we would be knocked out. At last the call came: all the matches had been played and we were still the highest-scoring losers – what's more, we had to leave for Cardiff within the next couple of hours!

In our next match, by the time we got to the final round, we were even further behind than we had previously been. We'd surely blown our desperately hoped-for second chance. How grim to bid farewell to the *Only Connect* studio, scene of my daydreams, without a taste of victory! At least I'd got some answers right this time, so I could leave with my head held – well, not exactly high, but not quite bent to the ground like an ostrich. The first category of the missing vowels round was 'Items required when driving a UK car in France'. Tom and Lydia had recently been driving in France, and, lightning-fingered, blazed through the category, and we were back on level terms! I buzzed in on the final question and got it wrong, losing us a point – but no matter, we'd won!

Next, to my astonishment, we defeated a team containing a *University Challenge* champion (who had entertained us backstage with impressions of Evelyn Waugh dismissing the work of Gertrude Stein and James Joyce as 'gibberish'), which saw us through to the quarter-finals. We won, lost and won again (the latter game a rematch against the team who'd beaten us in our opening episode) to propel us to the semi-final, where we improbably defeated a team of question-setters from *The Chase*.

I'd had to do last-minute shopping: I hadn't packed enough outfits, never expecting us to get so far. The first time I tried on the glossy shirt I'd bought on the off-chance we reached the final, the final was soon to start. It was far too tight, forcing my back into a hunch, my flesh bulging between the buttons like a stress ball through clenched fingers. Tom lent me a T-shirt to wear underneath it.

In the final, the subject of Mountweazels came up – fictitious entries in reference books used as copyright traps. I'd been researching Mountweazels for this very book (for a question I never used) and was able to rattle off a barrage of facts about them. It was exhilarating, the kind of moment that had hitherto only occurred in my wildest dreams. On the wall, I spotted that 'rabies' was an anagram of 'Serbia' – a fact I had discovered as a teenager when setting cryptic crosswords for my mum, a habit I'd taken up to ease my loneliness at boarding school, sending her my first cryptic crossword in a homemade letter sealed with honey.

I was sworn to secrecy about our victory. On the train back to Cambridge, I mouthed, 'We won!' to the cows in the fields we passed. One of the answers in the final had been 'We Are the Champions'; I listened to the song every day for about a month, my spirits soaring. For some time afterwards, I would find myself spontaneously chuckling and shaking my head in disbelief.

One Monday in March 2020, I was planning to present my quiz as usual, but reports of the spread of Covid were increasingly alarming, the headlines ever more outraged that the government hadn't closed pubs. I was plagued by the thought of letting down my contestants – I'd never cancelled a quiz before – but eventually called it off and posted the questions on Twitter instead. I didn't return to the pub until October the following year. During lockdown, Tom recruited me and Lydia to an online quiz league. I'd never been part of a quiz league before. The experience proved thrilling and terrifying. It was also very useful for identifying gaps in my knowledge. In hope of improving my performances, I recorded myself reciting facts for hours and listened to them whenever I left the house alone, repeating my own words in a determined murmur. It all slipped from my mind. I signed up to more and more online quiz leagues; I would grow jaded and overwhelmed by the amount of quizzing I was doing, would cut down, would feel bereft that I wasn't quizzing enough, and the cycle would begin again. I grew to feel part of a quizzing community vaster and more tight-knit than I'd ever imagined. It's predominantly composed of the loveliest people, partly, I think, because to be a good quizzer it helps to leave judgment and snobbery behind, to treat all information as equal no matter whether it relates to opera or soap opera, to geometry or Gene Autry.

I created an online version of my pub quiz, using Zoom. I sent my contestants a link to a webpage containing the questions, then dispatched teams to 'breakout rooms' to discuss them. As my quiz was written out for all to see, I was able to craft longer and more elaborate questions without the trouble of having to circumnavigate a pub repeating them several times to each team. One question I wrote was about a paragraph long and had the answer '*Sex and the City* and King Charles II'. As well as regulars from the pub, it attracted quiz obsessives and veterans of TV quiz shows. It was wonderful to witness how the fame of my sneaky questions had spread through the quiz world. Even when the quiz returned to the pub, I kept its online equivalent going; nowadays I often present the digital version with my youngest daughter in my arms.

This quiz book is largely drawn from questions I wrote during my first two seasons presenting The Mill's quiz. I'm rather proud of the quizzes within it and excited about springing them upon you!

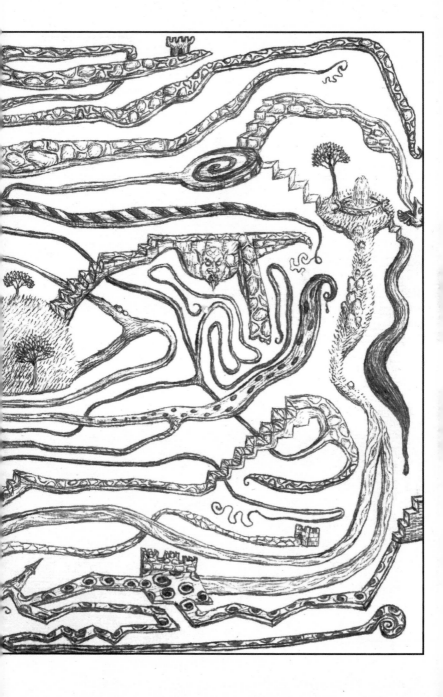

PART ONE:
ALL FUN AND GAMES

2

...Until Someone Loses An 'I'

Guess the words from their definitions. Each pair is spelt identically except that the second answer contains the letter 'i' at least once. For instance, 'a small mark and a fool' would lead to 'dot' and 'idiot'. Have half a point for each word in each pair.

1. A member of an ethnic group in North Africa and a disease that affects the heart and nerves

2. Enjoy the taste or smell of and someone who brings salvation

3. A member of the Addams Family and more lively

4. The second word of the SAS's three-word motto and places where milk products are processed

5. A palindromic word meaning 'pertain' or 'turn one's attention' and a palindromic word meaning 'someone who treats an abstract concept as if it had material existence'

6. A device used to hold something in position and the quality of being hirsute

7. Seize hold of by pulling and most sinewy

8. A city in the west of France and vapid things

This round is out of 8.

REBUS: GAMES

Each set of visual clues, read aloud, will combine to form the name of a sport or game. Identify the games.

1.

2.

3.

4.

5.

6.

7.

8.

This round is out of 8.

HUNT THE SYNONYMS

In this round (one of my less fiendish ones), change one letter of each word to make pairs of synonyms, e.g. 'Convert and gunnery' could be changed to 'Convent and nunnery'. Have one point per answer (half a point for each word).

1. Mistress and buffering
2. Paid and dug
3. Engage and maiden
4. Sacked and hole
5. Charm and gull
6. Aware and prime
7. Pertain and surf
8. Delicate and denote

This round is out of 8.

IF THIS IS THE ANSWER, WHAT'S THE QUESTION?

1. Martha finally admits that she is, after she and her husband demonstrate the acrimony of their relationship in front of two increasingly uncomfortable guests.

2. It was Judge Doom, who achieved this by faking an affair between Jessica and Acme, then having Acme killed.

3. 'Yes, unless you're referring to the leader of either the Coptic or the Greek Orthodox Church of Alexandria,' is one response to this sarcastic question, used to indicate that the answer to a previous question is obvious.

4. It was the latter, geneticists have concluded, though Aristotle believed that both had always existed.

5. No answer is provided to this riddle, found in a novel of 1865, though it has been suggested that 'Poe wrote on both' would be a valid response.

6. The answer to this question, asked in 1981, depends on whether you stop giving mixed messages and say you are mine, but trouble will ensue whatever the outcome.

7. It was behind a mail truck all along, after a search for it culminated in a confrontation with a giant alien.

8. According to an environmental conservation officer in America, the solution to this tongue-twister is 'about 700 pounds on a good day with the wind at his back'.

This round is out of 8.

DOCTOR, DOCTOR

I've selected eight real and fictional people who are all known as 'Doctor' and imagined what they might say to you if you consulted them for medical advice. Identify the eight people.

1. 'If you wish to remain healthy, on no account visit a city twenty-two miles south of Worcester and thirty-two miles north-east of Bristol. I caught hypothermia there after being submerged up to my waist in water, and I shall never return.'

2. 'I'm afraid I can't treat you now as I've just been woken by a call from four Scandinavians who want me to return and resume the love affair we engaged in during summertime.'

3. 'How sweet to be a medical practitioner, with the power of life and death over any man. I confess to having a mania for power, and mania is as priceless as genius. You must forgive me if my examination of you feels somewhat exotic. I have steel pincers instead of hands.'

4. 'Of course it's no problem you've called me out at three a.m. – I'm here for anyone in need at any time. Now, are you feeling down? If so, let's pick you up. I've brought my special cup for you to take a sip from.'

5. 'This medicinal omelette will cure your cold, and there's no reason to imagine it'll turn you into an evil brainwashed ninja obedient to my every whim! What the heck? Someone's dashed in and stolen the omelette! I hate that hedgehog!'

6. 'Now, my good fellow, you are suffering from nothing more than – but I am seized by nausea! Leave my sight, for I feel myself transforming without the aid of the draught I concocted, and my soul is boiling with causeless hatreds!'

7. 'I can't hear myself think with your snuffles and sniffs
   And your ningle-nose nurgles and puff-peffer-piffs!
   Take this puckberry pill and your nose and your chest
   Will be clear north and south! Will be clear east and west!'

8. 'I see you suffer from a neurological disorder. I have some sympathy for your situation as I myself am affected by alien hand syndrome. But such trifles will be easily overlooked in the mineshaft in which we and future generations will prosper to avoid the impending radioactivity.'

This round is out of 8.

WHAT'S THE DIFFERENCE? (NO. 1)

The questions in this round come in the form of jokes where the answer involves a spoonerism. For instance, if the question were 'What's the difference between a lovely glove and a small, silent cat?', the answer would be 'One's a cute mitten and the other's a mute kitten.'

1. What's the difference between a martial arts star and unpackaged French cheese?

2. What's the difference between completely false information and no filled pastries?

3. What's the difference between an intrigued visitor to our shores and someone angrily holding an inquest into a death?

4. What's the difference between a polymath and every disreputable woman's path?

5. What's the difference between what may be Metallica's most celebrated album and someone who preaches to Kermit and Miss Piggy?

6. What's the difference between the jewellery of a painted girl and an aristocratic Peeping Tom?

7. What's the difference between a comedy starring Diane Keaton and Bette Midler and the most incompetent group of players of a sport associated with public schools?

8. What's the difference between an eighteenth-century novel and many sets of little stones belonging to the heroine of *The Mill on the Floss*?

This round is out of 8.

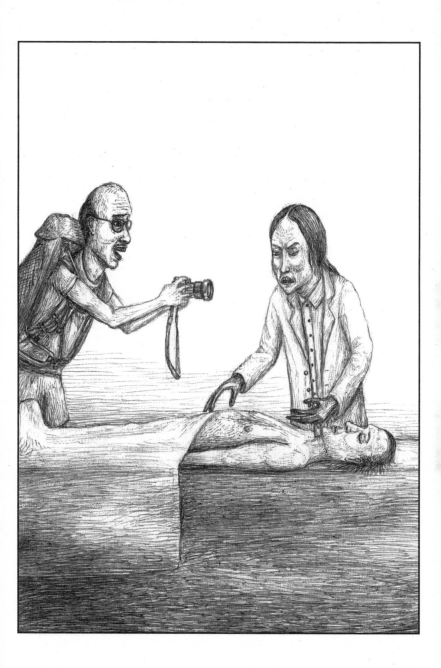

Round the World Trick or Treat

Identify these countries from the descriptions of their supernaturally themed festivals and traditions. But beware – you must also identify which four of the questions are 'tricks', where the described festivals or traditions are fabrications and belong to no country at all.

1. The Bon Festival, also known as the Obon Festival, is an annual Buddhist festival in this country, during which it is believed that the spirits of one's ancestors return to visit their relatives. Those celebrating may perform a traditional dance around a specially erected tower called a *yagura*.

2. In this country, Halloween celebrations traditionally involve theatre and dance performances themed around cricket, playing on the fact that the most widely spoken language uses the same word for 'vampire' and 'umpire'. The most popular drama is a re-enactment of the country's famous 1976 victory over Australia, with the home team bravely defending themselves not only against the Australians' spin bowling but the attacks of the vampiric umpire.

3. Barmbrack is traditionally served on Halloween in this country, which is said to be the birthplace of Halloween. It is a fruit cake which may have various objects baked inside it, which supposedly foretell the future of those who discover them. A coin symbolises wealth, a ring symbolises marriage in the near future and a thimble symbolises spinsterhood.

4. A winter festival in this country involves *kachela*, a dish of noodles in a cardamom-infused broth, and the warning that, if children have been ill-behaved the previous year, the Mackenhutch will creep in and steal their toes. The Mackenhutch is a figure derived from Sir Mackenzie Hutch, a notorious colonial governor overthrown during the 1803 War of Independence.

5. Ancient religious traditions in this country, though largely displaced by Methodist Christianity, hold that the god Chengu created the world by weeping six tears, each of which has a feast day dedicated to it. From the first tear sprouted Mount Aseru, the country's highest peak, and from the sixth tear all the monsters of the Earth were born.

6. In this country, on the night of 30th April to 1st May, witches are said to gather on the Brocken, the highest peak of the Harz Mountains. The mountain's association with witchcraft was alluded to by the country's most celebrated poet and dramatist, who tells of a journey to the Brocken in the lines, 'So over the valleys our company floats,/With witches a-farting on stinking old goats.'

7. American-style Halloween celebrations have grown popular in this country, displacing the increasingly rare festival of *pangangaluluwa*, which is confined to a few rural areas. In *pangangaluluwa* children pose as ghosts and go from house to house singing and demanding food or money, with the implied threat that they will steal the household's chickens and eggs if their demands are not met. All Saints' Day, known as Undas or Todos los Santos, is also celebrated.

8. Every August in this country, the sport of *ton ithmiang* is played, in which each participant assumes the role of a dead ancestor and attempts to catch a ribbon tied to the tail of a yak, with successful players supposedly ensuring their ancestor's safe passage through the afterlife. The sport has undergone a recent revival owing to *The Girl from Taghorang*, a hit TV costume drama about a girl who disguises herself as a man so that she can play the game and ensure a safe afterlife for her murdered father.

This round is out of 8.

Pros and Cons

Guess each pair of words from their definitions. Each pair of words is spelt identically except that one begins with 'pro' and the other with 'con' (for instance, 'professor' and 'confessor'). Have one point for each pair successfully guessed.

1. Part of a country or empire and cause someone to believe something

2. An expression of objection and competition

3. Movement forwards and a formal meeting or legislative body

4. Intense or penetrating beyond the superficial and bewilder

5. Plentiful and bewilder

6. The result of labour and behaviour

7. A group moving forwards in an orderly fashion and a reduction in price for a specific group of customers

8. Forbidding and compulsory enlistment

This round is out of 8.

Sum Fun with Roman Numerals

Identify the pairs of words from the following 'sums' which contain their definitions; in each case, the second word is spelt identically to the first word except for the addition of a letter or letters which form the equivalent in Roman numerals of the number in the 'sum'. For example, 'objectionably sentimental + 55 = a dozen' would lead to 'twee + LV = twelve'. Have a point for each pair of words successfully guessed.

1. A growth that can form on the body + 151 = someone who propels a vehicle

2. Bambi, for example + 54 = carry or transfer to someone

3. Carry or transfer to someone + 40 = in an outwardly bulging manner

4. A small bed + 2,001 = perpetrate

5. A South African with Dutch or Huguenot ancestry + 10 = fighter or dog

6. Hit with a whip + 6 = luxurious

7. Words extracted from someone else's speech or writing + 9 = a literary Don

8. Force + 2,000 = trade

This round is out of 8.

MONOPOLY

This round concluded the final quiz of the 2015–16 season, before the pub took its long summer holiday from quizzes. It was originally accompanied by a scoring system which enabled teams to gamble for extra points, but which could leave them with minus points if their gambles backfired. Teams could 'buy' **a maximum of three** properties in exchange for points **before the round started**, and would then be rewarded if they correctly answered a question on a property they 'owned'. **Old Kent Road** and **Whitechapel Road** each cost **1 point to buy** and were worth **2 ½ points** if they were subsequently answered correctly; **Water Works** and **Electric Company** each cost **1 ½ points to buy** and were worth **3 ½ points** if they were subsequently answered correctly; **Fleet Street** and **Strand** each cost **2 points to buy** and were worth **4 ½ points** if they were subsequently answered correctly; and **Park Lane** and **Mayfair** each cost **3 points to buy** and were worth **6 points** if they were subsequently answered correctly. The same property could be bought by more than one team, and teams would gain the usual point per correct answer on any property they did not own. The cost of purchased properties would be deducted from a team's score whether they had answered correctly or not – which caught out a few teams who assumed that a correct answer saw the cost of purchase returned along with the bonus points. For instance, if a team bought Whitechapel Road, Electric Company and Park Lane and got every question of the round right apart from Park Lane, they would gain a total of 5 ½ points for the round (5 for the questions they got right on properties they didn't own, plus 6 for getting Whitechapel Road and Electric Company right, minus 5 ½ for the costs of all their properties). The time it took me to explain the rules of this round meant that this particular quiz wildly over-ran, and my subsequent attempts to finish it at breakneck speed rather punctured the dramatic finale I had hoped for. Nonetheless, you're very welcome to try it with the scoring system yourself or spring it on your friends, family and enemies.

Old Kent Road – Which cathedral town in Kent received city status in 1211 but lost it in 1998, apparently owing to an administrative mix-up?

Whitechapel Road – The Whitechapel Gallery presented the first major show in Britain of which painter, whose tools included syringes and whose painting *No. 5, 1948* was sold in 2006 for a record-breaking sum?

Water Works – In 1990 Hattie Hasan founded a firm of female plumbers by what name? It is named after a type of valve.

Electric Company – Jack Cover is best known for which invention, named in honour of an adventure novel in which the teenage hero Tom Swift, whom Cover referred to as Thomas A. Swift, creates an electric rifle and takes it on an expedition in Africa?

Fleet Street – Which 1970s TV series derived its title from the Cockney rhyming slang for the Flying Squad?

Strand – On the last weekend of February 2016, the branch of Pizza Hut on the Strand, along with a handful of other UK branches, offered free pizza to customers called Charlotte, Tom, Eddie, Christian, Mark and Kate. What, specifically, was this intended to celebrate?

Park Lane – Which resident of Park Lane, who died in 2023, financed the film *Unlawful Killing*, an examination of deaths which, according to the film, were partly orchestrated by a couple that the film describes as 'a Fred West-style psychopath' and 'a gangster in a tiara'?

Mayfair – Patrick Hamilton inserted one letter into the name of a Mayfair location to form the punning title of a novel about a borderline alcoholic. What is the novel called? [Hint: the title has two words, the extra letter having been inserted into the first word.]

This round is out of 8 if played conventionally, or could get you anywhere between minus 8 and 13½ points if played according to the more complex scoring system.

WHAT'S THE DIFFERENCE? (NO. 2)

The questions in this round come in the form of jokes where the answer involves a spoonerism. For instance, if the question were 'What's the difference between a lovely glove and a small, silent cat?', the answer would be 'One's a cute mitten and the other's a mute kitten.'

1. What's the difference between a lack of creative inspiration and a contemptible person's granite?

2. What's the difference between an enquiry about the nature of being and a Biblical character who is turned into a pillar of salt?

3. What's the difference between a star of silent comedies and the result of the Battle of Little Bighorn?

4. What's the difference between a slot in a door and improved ways to keep a door closed?

5. What's the difference between a method of transmitting information developed in the nineteenth century and an uncouth method?

6. What's the difference between the name of a former British colony on the Gulf of Guinea and a wintry apparition?

7. What's the difference between the sensation of being in a high-pressure situation and a chiropodist's job description?

8. What's the difference between the first ever UK number one single whose title was phrased as a question and an enquiry into the extent to which a cat on display might originate from the Netherlands?

This round is out of 8.

PART TWO:

GENERAL
FIENDISHNESS

A Soft Pilchard Towel

Each answer in this round is an anagram of a capital city; in each case give the original answer for half a point and the country of which its anagram is capital for another half-point.

1. Which surname is shared by a major character from *The Man From U.N.C.L.E.* and a major character from *Star Wars*?

2. In which country would you find Timbuktu?

3. Hassall, Powell, Doherty: who is missing from this line-up?

4. Which island, about 90 miles south-east of Grenada, is sometimes thought to derive its name from its cigar-like shape?

5. Who is the drummer in the band Dr. Teeth and the Electric Mayhem?

6. The name of which creature can follow the words head, whale or wood?

7. In a flower, which word refers to the part of the stamen that contains pollen?

8. Finland contains an estimated two million what, which may be electric, smoke or mobile?

This round is out of 8.

*   The title of this round is an anagram of 'Capitals of the world'.

29

REBUS: MUSIC MAKERS

Each set of visual clues, read aloud, will combine to form the name of a musician or band. (For example, a picture of Morris dancers followed by a picture of the sea would form 'Morrissey.') Identify the eight musicians and bands.

5.

6.

7.

8.

This round is out of 8.

PREMATURE OBITUARIES

1. 'His films inspired intense reactions; several were cult classics with devoted followings, but they were generally flawed enough to inspire loathing from those not on the same bawdy, anarchical comedy wavelength' is an extract from the obituary of which American-born director, which was erroneously published by *Variety* in 2015?

2. In 2003, it was discovered that *CNN*'s website included several obituaries for people who were still living, some of which contained fragments from other people's obituaries. For instance, Fidel Castro was described as a 'lifeguard, athlete, movie star' in a reference to which other world leader, who was to die the following year?

3. *CNN*'s website also described Pope John Paul II as having a 'love of racing' and Dick Cheney as being 'the UK's favorite grandmother', both of which came from the template of whose obituary, who died in 2002?

4. Whose premature obituary, erroneously published after the death of his brother Ludwig, is rumoured to have been what led him to bequeath most of his fortune to the recognition of human endeavour in an attempt to change posterity's opinion of him?

5. Which actor, famed for his voice acting, was pronounced dead during a 1998 radio broadcast, as the announcer had him confused with the man convicted of assassinating Martin Luther King, with whom he shares his first and middle names?

6. Which Jamaican advocate of Pan-Africanism, who was the subject of an album by Burning Spear, died of a stroke apparently induced by the shock of reading his own erroneously published obituary, which described him as having died 'broke, alone and unpopular'?

7. Which American musician, born Vincent Furnier, was the subject of a spoof obituary in a 1973 *Melody Maker* article claiming he had been killed by a faulty guillotine in his stage act?

8. Which American novelist was the subject of premature obituaries after he and his wife were involved in two plane crashes in two days in 1954? He described how he and his wife preserved the obituaries in two scrapbooks, one covered with zebra hide and the other with lion skin, and announced his intention 'to read them at least once a year in order to keep my morale up to par when the critics have recovered their aplomb and return to the assault.'

This round is out of 8.

GENERAL FIENDISHNESS (NO. 1)

1. 'Don't know the manners of good society, eh? Well, I guess I know enough to turn you inside out, old gal – you sockdologizing old man-trap' are thought to have been the last words ever heard by which famous American?

2. Which eight-letter word, defined as 'people who are very skilled, particularly in an ostentatious way' consists of the same four letters repeated in the same order?

3. A promotion for the Guinness World Records website, which was at the time the world's smallest advertisement, was fastened to which proverbially excellent animal part?

4. *Aegilops*, the name of a genus of grasses, is said to be the longest word in the English language with what characteristic?

5. In 1888, police were summoned after a woman in the French city of Arles was presented with what, allegedly accompanied by the instructions 'Guard this object carefully'?

6. The humorous unit of one millihelen is defined as the quantity of beauty required to do what?

7. Which song, a reworking of a Cuban original, was intended to be used at the 2000 Democratic National Convention, a move which was abandoned because the first line of its chorus was too reminiscent of a scandal which had surfaced two years earlier?

8. The film *Muppets Most Wanted* features a cameo by which singer playing a man who shows people where to sit at a wedding, as well as a cameo by which Austrian-German actor performing a dance in triple time (half a point for each)?

This round is out of 8.

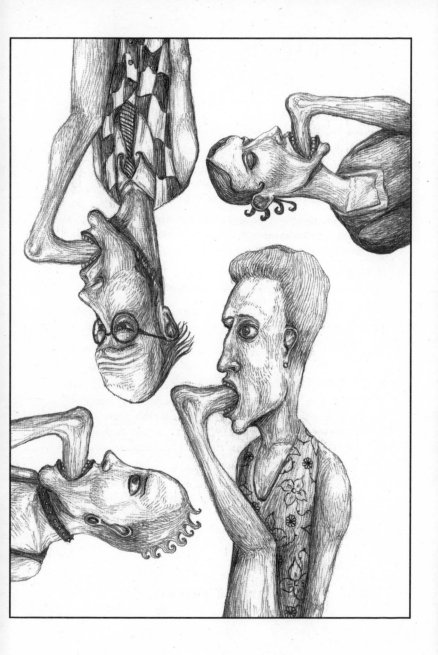

FOOT IN MOUTH

Here is a round on the Foot in Mouth awards, bestowed annually by the Plain English Campaign for 'a baffling comment by a public figure'.

1. Who won the 1999 award after attempting to explain comments he had made that would cost him his job with the words, 'At this moment in time, if that changes in years to come I don't know, but what happens here today and changes as we go along, that is part of life's learning and part of your inner beliefs. But at this moment in time I did not say them things and at the end of the day I want to put that on record because it has hurt people'?

2. Which actress became the youngest winner of the award when she won it in 2000? Fourteen years later she published a guide to pregnancy and parenting, which warned of the dangers of tampons, nappies and vaccinations. It attracted criticism, much of which used the title of her most famous film to describe her.

3. Which former footballer, a cousin of Frank Lampard, won the 2010 award for his gaffes when commentating, such as 'These balls now – they literally explode off your feet'?

4. 'I believe in an America where millions of Americans believe in an America that's the America millions of Americans believe in. That's the America I love,' was among the comments invoked by the Plain English Campaign to justify giving which presidential candidate the 2012 award? (The Plain English Campaign may have done this man a disservice here: the quotation comes from an article in the *National Review* by conservative commentator Mark Steyn, who appears to have been mocking the kind of language used by this man's speechwriters rather than quoting him directly.)

5. Which English model, who has on more than one occasion pleaded guilty to assaulting her employees with telephones, won the 2006 award for saying, 'I love England, especially the food. There's nothing I like more than a lovely bowl of pasta'?

6. 'When it comes to words I have a uniqueness that I find almost impossible in terms of art – and it's my words that actually make my art quite unique' were the words that won whom the 2001 award? She was once described by David Bowie as 'William Blake as a woman, written by Mike Leigh'.

7. Silvio Berlusconi won the 2008 award for his description of which person, who was at the time preparing to undertake a new job, as 'handsome, young and suntanned'?

8. A marketer named Nick Underwood won the 1997 award after the *Daily Express* quoted him as commenting, 'In life, there are all colours and the _____ are a reflection of that… There are no nationalities in the _____ – they are techno-babies, but they are supposed to reflect life in that sense'. The name of which popular quartet fills both blank spaces?

This round is out of 8.

THE ONE AND ONLY

1. Which African nation is the only country in the world which contains all five vowels once and only once? It is also, of all the countries in the world with one-word names, the one with the highest *Scrabble* score (that is to say, if it were a valid *Scrabble* word and bonus squares were not taken into account).

2. Which is the only country in the world named after a woman? (This does not include Ireland, which is thought to be named after the goddess Ériu.)

3. The Austrian Adam Rainer developed acromegaly in his twenties, making him the only person in recorded medical history to have been both what and what?

4. Who was the only fictional character to make *Time* magazine's list of the 100 most influential people of the twentieth century? The magazine described him as '[t]his young scamp — with his paper bag-shaped head…'

5. Named after a Charles Kingsley novel, which Devon village has the only British place name to contain an exclamation mark?

6. Which actress and singer won an Oscar in 1972, making her the only Oscar winner in history whose parents also both won Oscars, and whose mother would go on to be depicted in an Oscar-winning performance?

7. Peter, the Lord's cat, also known as the Marylebone mog, was the only non-human to receive an obituary in which reference book?

8. Elizabeth Barton, a Catholic nun and soothsayer who condemned the marriage of Henry VIII and Anne Boleyn, was the only woman in English history to have been given which posthumous dishonour, a fate she shared with William Wallace and Thomas More?

This round is out of 8.

GENERAL FIENDISHNESS (NO. 2)

1. Which name may be placed before or after a capital city to produce a great American composer and a great American writer respectively?

2. The name of which fish acquired a whole new meaning when it appeared in the title of a Beastie Boys song containing the lyric '#1 on the side and don't touch the back'?

3. The marine biologist Stephen Hillenburg is best known as the creator of which American TV series, which first aired in 1999?

4. 247 years apart, two authors named Fielding published hit novels featuring a title character with what surname?

5. Which term for sleep is also the name of a place to which, according to the Book of Genesis, Cain was banished after murdering his brother?

6. What is the smallest four-digit prime number, as well as the largest number to make a valid English word when written in Roman numerals?

7. Cabbaged, baggaged and the plant families Fagaceae and Fabaceae are four of the five eight-letter words which can be played on a musical instrument (that is to say, using the letters A to G). Which word, defined as 'subjected to a humiliating act', is the fifth?

8. The petrel, if the theory that it was named after St Peter is correct, received its name for the same reason that the Jesus lizard is named after Jesus. What characteristic do these two creatures and these two holy men supposedly share?

This round is out of 8.

THE OSCARS

In this round, each answer is a real-life or fictitious person who was portrayed in an Oscar-winning performance. Name the people (for half a point each) and the actors who won Oscars for portraying them (for another half a point each).

1. Which singer, who died in 2004, liked to point out his 'three nos': 'No dog, no cane, no guitar'?

2. Which author, one of whose works was adapted into a 1961 Blake Edwards film, is thought to have been the basis for the character Dill in *To Kill a Mockingbird*?

3. The official title of which leader, who died in 2003, began with the words His Excellency President for Life, Field Marshal Al Hadji Doctor?

4. 'She thrums with purpose when she writes. Her scattershot joy and frantic distraction refocus, and she funnels into her purest form'. This is Priya Parmar's description of whom in her novel *Vanessa and Her Sister*?

5. Who was the first person to be awarded the title Defender of the Faith by a Pope because of a treatise ascribed to him which attacked his contemporary Martin Luther, though he was stripped of this title by the next Pope?

6. The Jasper Fforde novel *Something Rotten*, in which the worlds of literature and reality converge, features which character outlining his approach to difficult situations with the words, 'Pretend to be mad and talk a lot. Then — and this is the important bit — do *nothing at all* until you absolutely have to and then make sure everyone dies'?

7. Who was queen consort first of France and then of England, and acted as regent when her son Richard went on the Third Crusade?

8. 'She has the eyes of Stalin and the voice of Marilyn Monroe'* was French President François Mitterrand's assessment of whom?

This round is out of 8.

....

*   This is more commonly quoted as 'The eyes of Caligula...' but Jacques Attali, a former aide to Mitterrand, insists that it was Stalin the French president was referring to. I originally tried illustrating this with a portrait of Marilyn Monroe bearing the eyes and eyebrows of Stalin, but the result looked so eerily like Madonna that I began to harbour suspicions about Madonna's parentage.

LOST IN TRANSLATION*

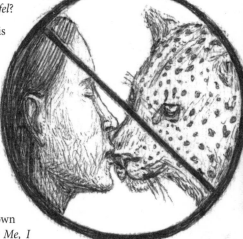

1. Which 1999 film is known in Japan as *17-Year-Old Girl's Medical Chart*?

2. Which 2009 film is known in Israel as *It's Raining Falafel*?

3. Which 1938 film is known in Germany as *One Does Not Kiss Leopards*?

4. Which 1968 film is known in Italy as *Please Don't Touch the Old Women*?

5. Which 1989 film is known in Spain as *This Dead Man is Very Alive*?

6. Which 2004 film is known in Italy as *If You Leave Me, I Delete You*?

7. Which 1959 film is known in Russia as *In Jazz There are Only Girls*?

8. Which 1973 film is known in Argentina as *Shocking Red Venice*?

This round is out of 8.

....

* When researching this round, I'd been tickled to discover several particularly juicy titles from China – which were revealed, upon further investigation, to be hoaxes. They included *Batman and Robin* rendered as *Come to My Cave and Wear this Rubber Codpiece, Cute Boy*; *Field of Dreams* as *Imaginary Dead Ball Players Live in My Cornfield*; and *Babe* as *The Happy Dumpling-to-be Who Talks and Solves Agricultural Problems* – all of which were dreamt up by the website topfive.com and reported as true by *The New York Times*, *ABC* and *CNN*.

REBUS: THE BEATLES

These visual clues, read aloud, will combine to form the names of seven Beatles songs. Identify them.

1.

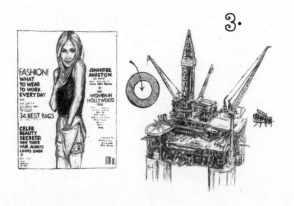

2.

3.

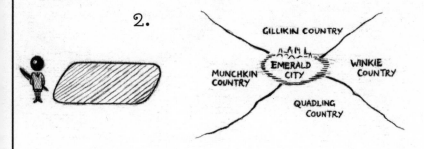

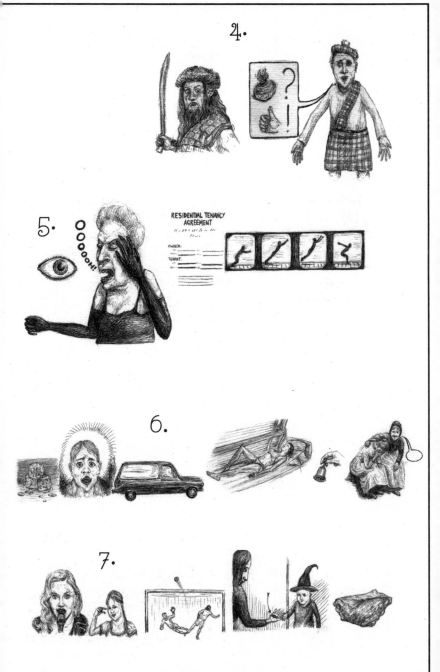

This round is out of 7.

GENERAL FIENDISHNESS (NO. 3)

1. Which type of wool takes its name from an old name for a city which is currently the capital of a country bordering Iraq?

2. Jared Hess used which former pseudonym of Elvis Costello as the title of a 2004 film? Costello refused to believe Hess's claim that this was a coincidence, commenting, 'Maybe somebody told him the name and he truly feels that he came about it by chance. But it's two words that you're never going to hear together.'

3. Lisa Lindahl was inspired to invent the sports bra after her sister suggested that women needed an equivalent of what item? The first sports bra was made by sewing two of these items together.

4. In 1901, Annie Edson Taylor became the first person to do what, which she hoped would bring her wealth and fame? Wealth did not materialise, as her manager absconded with the container she had used and she spent most of her savings attempting to track it down.

5. When Paul Simon met the composer Pierre Boulez, what did Boulez mistakenly do that inspired one of Simon's most famous songs?

6. 'Brain freeze' was added to what in 2004 following the results of a poll?

7. Which item of stationery is known in France as a trombone?

8. The older brother of Popeye's girlfriend Olive Oyl has what first name, which he shares with one of the sons of Leda in Greek mythology?

This round is out of 8.

NAMESAKES

1. Which Scotsman described his namesake as 'the bane of my life. He's a remarkable young man and does a remarkable job, but it is irritating to keep being confused with him: "Can you come on TV and discuss quantum physics?"' His namesake responded on Twitter with the words, 'I'm the bane of his life! He should see the look on my face when I turn up and they expect me to play Hamlet!'

2. A man with what name described how his life had been particularly affected since the 2009 MTV Video Music Awards? He described the fan mail he receives as 'a great confidence booster. It's like endless amounts of, "You're beautiful, you're so talented, you're a great role model, you have a beautiful voice," and here I am just like, "Oh, thank you!"'

3. Who wrote the novel *Mrs Palfrey at the Claremont*? It features the alcoholic character Mrs Burton, who is thought to have been a mischievous reference to the author's namesake.

4. In his memoir *Back Story*, which comedian recalled being mistaken for his namesake by David Miliband, who complimented him on his novels?

5. According to an article in the *Guardian*, who, when studying film-making at Goldsmiths, liked to joke that one day he would become more famous than his actor namesake?

6. In the series *The Royals*, Elizabeth Hurley plays a queen consort who shares her name with a queen of Adiabene whose story is related by Josephus. The husband of Hurley's character is succeeded as king by Jake Maskall's character, who shares his name with a king who founded the Achaemenid Empire. The names of both of these characters are connected (in different ways) to which US state?

7.   In 2012, after a character in a TV series was shown arriving at a Howard Johnson hotel with his new wife Megan and discovering that the pool was closed, the hotel chain (in real life) offered to make amends by granting anyone with the same first name and surname as the TV character a free one-night stay. What is the character's name?

8.   'One interviewer even asked me if I kissed girls. He was a guy and, yes, it was super awkward,' said a marketing manager by what name? It is pronounced identically to a stage name adopted by a singer to avoid confusion with a star of the film *Almost Famous*.

This round is out of 8.

The Mail and the Masterpieces

Identify these books and their authors, which have been reimagined as Daily Mail-*style headlines. Have half a point for the title and half for the author.*

1. Whitby's plague of horrific attacks: the sinister link to Eastern European migration

2. Adding insult to injury! Renowned car enthusiast flees harrowing jail ordeal... only to find ancestral home overrun with SQUATTERS

3. Country lass Catherine shows off her figure as she slinks into Gimmerton Chapel in chic wedding dress – but rumours of her feelings for her gypsy ex just won't go away

4. Too boggy for the bobbies! Heir turns to junkie loner to thwart cousin's moorland murder plot that Scotland Yard were too clueless to investigate

5. Whinny ninny: retired surgeon spends all day nattering to HORSES! 'He was never like this before getting exposed to foreign cultures,' claims wife

6. How to reward an enormous man who prowls the streets at night manipulating YOUR children's dreams? With his own WINDSOR MANSION, of course – at taxpayers' expense

7. Sue Phillotson looks stylish as she steps out with husband in the wake of family tragedy – as rumours abound that the cousin she shared an illicit love nest with is back in HIS ex's saucy clutches

8. Not very ladylike! Lady Catherine caught launching astonishing rant at landowner's daughter rumoured to be cosying up to her nephew

This round is out of 8.

COOKING WITH THE STARS

1. 'Sisterly Translation' and 'Sweet Southern Memories' are chapters of which poet and autobiographer's first cookbook, entitled *Hallelujah! The Welcome Table*?

2. Which American singer released a cookbook called *If It Makes You Healthy*?

3. Which artist wrote in his 1973 cookbook *Les Dîners de Gala*, 'If I hate that detestable degrading vegetable called spinach it is because it is shapeless, like Liberty. [...] The opposite of shapeless spinach, is armour. I love eating suits of arms, in fact I love all shell fish...'

4. 'I'm-Gonna-Slap-You-With-My-Whisk Tomato Bisque' and 'Your Ribs Is Too Short to Box With God' are recipes from the cookbook of which rapper and *Celebrity Big Brother* contestant?

5. Which Russian-born actor's cookbook is subtitled *Food Fit for the King and You*?

6. Whose vegan cookbook, *The Kind Diet*, contains not only recipes but personal anecdotes, including how she was chased by paparazzi yelling 'Fatgirl!' while preparing for a film role?

7. Who, in 1970, published a cookbook subtitled *Hundreds of Delicious Recipes For You From His Seven Dining Rooms*, the cover of which depicted him posing amongst kitchen furniture designed to look like piano keyboards?

8. Whose Weight Watchers cookbook opens with an account of how the press taunted her when she gained weight, replacing the last word of her title with 'pork' to create a cruel nickname?

This round is out of 8.

REBUS: PROFESSIONS

Each set of visual clues, read aloud, will combine to form the name of a profession. Identify the seven professions.

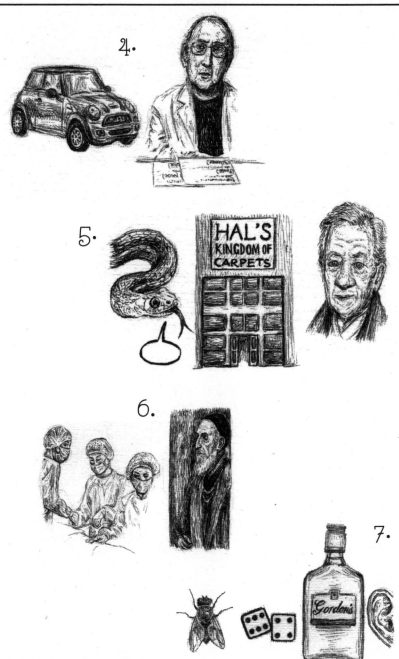

4.

5.

HAL'S KINGDOM OF CARPETS

6.

7.

This round is out of 7.

GENERAL FIENDISHNESS (NO. 4)

1. Which part of the body, the existence of which has never been definitively proved, is named after the German-born doctor Ernst Gräfenberg?

2. The animated TV character Norville Rogers and the Jamaican-American musician Orville Burrell are each better known by the same name. What is it?

3. Which word meaning 'relating to love' can be prefixed by three consecutive letters of the alphabet to make a word meaning 'libellous'?

4. The theme tune to which TV series features the same note being played over and over again to spell out the title character's surname?

5. The 2007 Charles Webb novel *Home School* is a sequel to which 1963 novel by the same author? The sequel is set in the mid-1970s and involves Benjamin enlisting his mother-in-law to seduce a school principal so he and his wife can blackmail the principal into letting them home-school their children.

6. The first six letters of which book of the Bible spell the name of a town in north-west England?

7. Alexis Texas was one name proposed for which fictional character, who first appeared in 2006?

8. An effigy of whom, his family's only son, was burnt after he intervened on behalf of his father, a Tory who was being shouted down during election hustings in Yorkshire in 1837? The effigy held a potato in one hand and a herring in the other, alluding to his Irish ancestry.

This round is out of 8.

IT TAKES TWO

In this round, each description can apply to two different answers. Have half a point for each answer in the pair.

1. This actress got her big break as an adolescent, playing a character taken under the wing of a gun-toting loner. She attended an Ivy League university and went on to win the Best Actress Oscar. Her feature directorial debut was a film in which she played the mother of a young boy.

2. This band was formed in 1983 by two brothers with the surname Reid. It made the top 20 in a poll run by *The List* magazine to find the 50 greatest Scottish bands of all time.

3. This Bafta-nominated BBC TV comedy series was first broadcast in the 1990s. Its theme tune is a cover of the ABBA song which gives the programme its title.

4. This song was jointly named 'Best British Pop Single 1952–1977' at the British Record Industry Britannia Awards ceremony. The fandango is mentioned in its lyrics.

5. Under the headline 'Heroines as ruthless as they are alluring', a *New York Times* article names the title character of this German-language twentieth-century opera, adapted from the work of a dramatist who was controversial in his time, as an exception to the rule that opera heroines 'often seem born to suffer' (which may strike the reader as an odd observation, as the opera's title character is violently killed at its conclusion). The opera shares its name with a joint winner of the 1969 Eurovision Song Contest.

6. This striker has been named in the PFA Premier League Team of the Year and has represented his country, including at the 2010 and 2014 FIFA World Cups. He spent several years at Atlético Madrid and on his forearm he has a tattoo of his own name in Tengwar, a writing system invented by J. R. R. Tolkien.

7. In a 2012 YouGov survey for *Prospect* magazine, this politician was named as one of the fifteen most admired British people alive. If a vowel is placed before the last letter of the politician's surname, the surname becomes the name of an African country.

8. This British actor was born in the early 1960s and appeared in the TV series *Vanity Fair* and *Doc Martin*. If one letter is removed from the actor's surname, it becomes a word for 'Monday' in a European language.

This round is out of 8.

MOTION PICTURE MIXTURE

Each word of these phrases is the first word of the title of a film, with the films that make up each phrase having a featured actor in common (which may include voice performances). Identify the eight actors. For instance, the sentence **Dirty, Mean Little Midnight Mary, Killing Everybody's Joy** *would provide the answer 'Robert de Niro' (the films in question being* Dirty Grandpa; Mean Streets; Little Fockers; Midnight Run; Mary Shelley's Frankenstein; Killing Season; Everybody's Fine; *and* Joy*).*

1. Morning Rooster Suddenly Bringing Love On Adam's Little Desk.

2. Toy Angels Sully That Extremely Big Cloud.

3. It's Still Falling Out, Dancing Into Dark, Fantastic Death.

4. Little Steve, Eternal Revolutionary, All Hideous, Holy, Heavenly Carnage!

5. Cold, Dead Rabbit Before My Eyes? Happy Birthday!

6. Batman, Kiss Lucky Robin, Driving Along London High Street.

7. Mystic August, Sleeping Fireflies. I Eat My Mother's Mirror.

8. Our Father, Great, Kind Star Barnacle, Murder Hitler.

This round is out of 8.

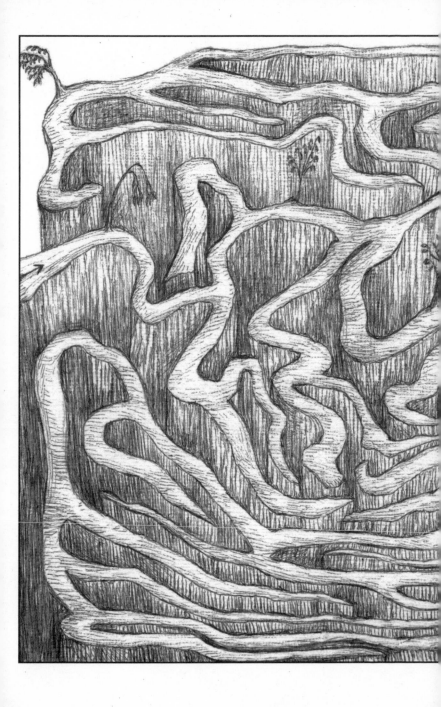

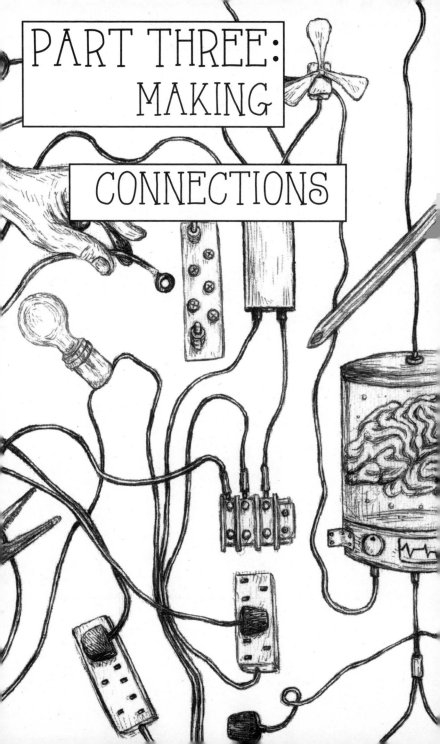

PART THREE:
MAKING

CONNECTIONS

SPOT THE LINK (NO. 1)

1. The only country in the world named after a chemical element is named after which element?

2. Which word for part of an animal can be preceded by the word 'globe' to mean 'someone who travels widely'?

3. Which foodstuff can also be a term of endearment, the title of a Mariah Carey song or the first name of a film character played by Ursula Andress?

4. Which foodstuff can also be a term of endearment, the title of a System of a Down song or the first name of a film character played by Marilyn Monroe?

5. Which word for a plant used as an ingredient in absinthe becomes a word for the larvae of a beetle if the two halves of the word are swapped around?

6. The name of which container is shared in an idiomatic expression meaning 'to die' and a challenge, popular during 2014, intended to raise awareness of motor neurone disease?

7. If you add the letters 'ni' to the beginning of which four-letter word, you get another word with the same meaning?

8. What do these answers have in common?

This round is out of 8.

PICTURE CONNECTIONS

What do the following sets of pictures have in common? (Be as specific as possible. Hint: the pictures in question 7 are displayed in ascending order.)

1.

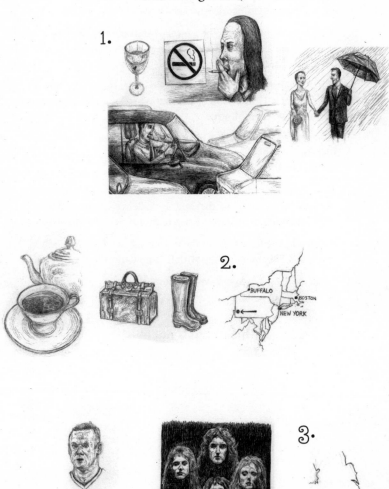

2.

3.

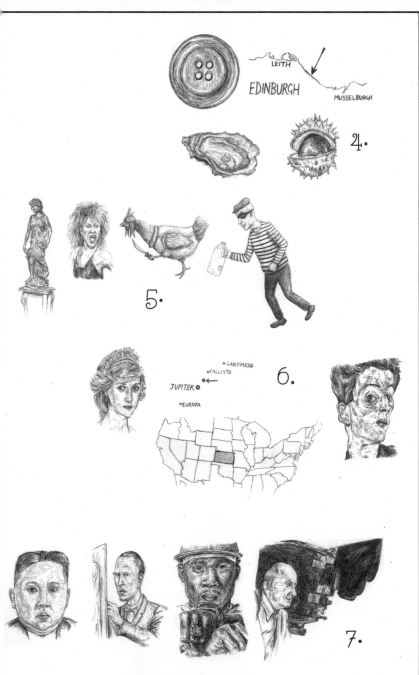

This round is out of 7.

IT'S ANALOGY SEASON! (NO. 1)

1. Semibreve is to whole note as crotchet is to what?

2. 'Are You Gonna Be My Girl' is to Paul McCartney and Wings as the 1982 song 'The Look of Love' is to which family band?

3. Transfer from a regular position for temporary duty elsewhere is to 1/3600 as very small is to which fraction?

4. Jane Austen and Catwoman are to William Shakespeare as Solitaire and Dr Quinn are to which monarch?

5. The letter X is to *Scarface* (the 1932 version) as which food is to *The Godfather*?

6. St Helier is to Trenton as which city is to Santa Fe?

7. Foxtrot is to a feather in my arms as alfa is to what?

8. Snow is to Sammy Cahn and Jule Styne as Bleed is to the Rolling Stones as what is to the Beatles?

This round is out of 8.

68

EIGHT DEGREES OF KEVIN BACON

Whom or what does each number represent?

Kevin Bacon appeared on **No. 1**, in an episode which showed his brother getting a makeover from the Fab Five. The Fab Five's Thom Filicia is a lover of **No. 2**, a condiment which, so he claimed in an interview, he had about six different types in his fridge. **No. 2** is also the stage name of the DJ Dijon McFarlane, who has collaborated on the song 'Don't Hurt Me' with **No. 3**. **No. 3**, whose alter egos include the Harajuku Barbie and Roman Zolanski, was born on the same island as the journalist and newsreader **No. 4**. In 1998 a book was published bringing together **No. 4**'s favourite poems, with **No. 5** among the poets featured. In 2007, to mark the 200th anniversary of one of **No. 5**'s most famous poems, Cumbria Tourism released a rap version of it, containing the lines: 'Must have been 10,000 I saw in my retina/No more than a glance then I register they're beautiful etcetera/I never knew in advance but they were tossing up their heads like a pogo dance'. The rapper who performed this version was dressed as a **No. 6**. Famous **No. 6**s include Nutkin and Timmy Tiptoes, both of whom are title characters of books by **No. 7**. **No. 7** has been portrayed on screen by **No. 8**, who appeared in the film *My One and Only* with Kevin Bacon.

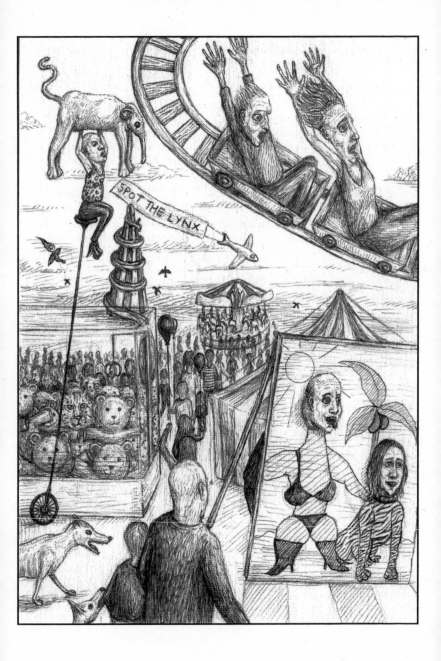

SPOT THE LINK (NO. 2)

1. What is the first name of Spider-Man's aunt as well as being the surname of a man fired by *Autocar* magazine in the 1990s after readers noticed a rude and irreverent message he had concealed in the first letters of texts he was editing?

2. Which word is shared in the name of a band whose albums include *Up On the Sun* and *Too High to Die*, the stage name of Michael Lee Aday and the title of the second studio album by The Smiths?

3. Which word can be an expression of surprise in English as well as meaning 'horn' in French and 'heart' in Latin?

4. Which surname is shared by an actress who won a Golden Globe for her performance in the film *The King and I* and an author whose books include *The Tiger Who Came to Tea*?

5. The name of which sparkling wine refers to the underground chambers in which it traditionally used to be stored?

6. Which word meaning 'thug' or 'yob' can mean 'hit' if it has a 'c' placed in front of it or 'disregard' if it has an 'f' placed in front of it?

7. Which word, derived from the phrase 'fall off', can refer to byproducts or waste material, and in particular parts of a butchered animal which are often removed when the animal is being prepared for consumption?

8. And what do these seven answers have in common?

This round is out of 8.

It's Analogy Season! (No. 2)

1. A cabinet in which to store reading material is to a legal or medical reference work detailing previous occurrences as a road which runs above another road is to which religious festival?

2. A 1999 UK number one for Blondie is to a 2000 US number one for Santana as a Booker Prize-winning novel by John Banville is to a Booker Prize-winning novel by whom?

3. Mrs Gren is to the processes of life as Roy G. Biv is to what?

4. The original couple are to credit as a domesticated carnivore and part of a skeleton are to which device?

5. The Italian flag is to the Hungarian flag as the French flag is to the flag of which country?

6. The Ant Hill Mob were to the Bulletproof Bomb as who were to the Mean Machine?

7. Goose is to thirty-five thousand and six as which bird is to five thousand one hundred and eighty-one?

8. Hitler was to 1938 as Stalin was to 1939 and 1942 as you were to which year? (You can have two years either way.)

This round is out of 8.

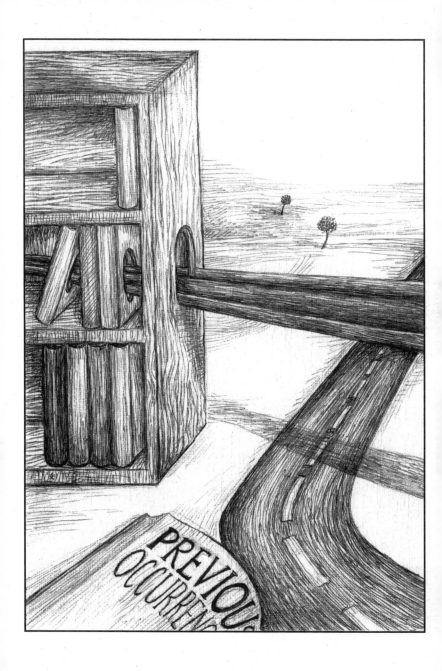

WHAT DO THE FOLLOWING HAVE IN COMMON? (NO. 1)

1. An actor who starred in *9½ Weeks* opposite Kim Basinger, the author of *Finnegans Wake*, an actor who played Tony in *Men Behaving Badly* and a former editor of the *Independent* who has presented various political and historical television programmes?

2. The Powerpuff Girls, Gaston Julia, the Phantom of the Opera and my malodorous dog?

3. Abdul Fakir, John Wayne, David Dickinson and Edward Kennedy Ellington?

4. A small hard seed in a fruit, notes sounded together, a forename shared by two men (one fictional and the other real) who had to leave their TV jobs after, respectively, obliviously reading out an offensive sign-off from a teleprompter and making a racist comment about Marcel Desailly, and a company which launched the Fantastic Four?

5. Platinum, shorthair, shindig and triggerman?

6. Nutwood, The Hundred Acre Wood, Jellystone National Park and 32 Windsor Gardens?

7. Chain, regalia, pains and Meg Ryan?

8. King Aethelred of Wessex, William Wordsworth, Jarvis Pennyworth and Walter Winterbottom?

This round is out of 8.

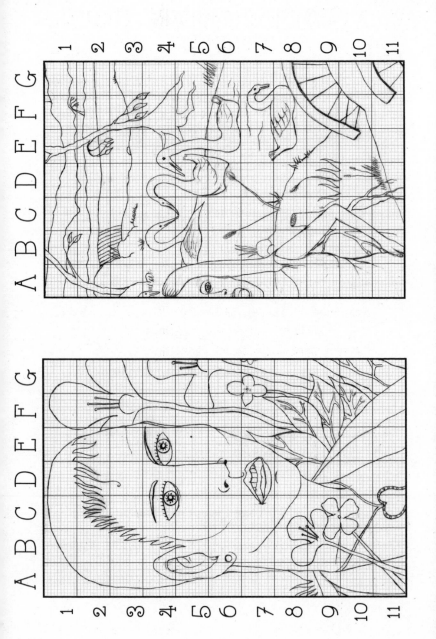

SPOT THE SIMILARITIES

Each of these pictures can be divided into 77 squares, each one indicated by a grid reference such as a1. Eight of the squares in Picture 1 are identical to squares in Picture 2, except that they have been rotated by 90° (either clockwise or anticlockwise) or 180°. Identify, by grid references, the eight squares which are identical in both pictures:

_____ in Picture 1 is identical to _____ in Picture 2.

_____ in Picture 1 is identical to _____ in Picture 2.

_____ in Picture 1 is identical to _____ in Picture 2.

_____ in Picture 1 is identical to _____ in Picture 2.

_____ in Picture 1 is identical to _____ in Picture 2.

_____ in Picture 1 is identical to _____ in Picture 2.

_____ in Picture 1 is identical to _____ in Picture 2.

_____ in Picture 1 is identical to _____ in Picture 2.

This round is out of 8.

IT'S ANALOGY SEASON! (NO. 3)

1. Geoff or Damien is to the highest degree as which former archbishop is to a lesser result?

2. Enthusiastic flying creature is to tofu as furry creature's entrance or exit is to which item of clothing?

3. Marten is to a German philosopher and economist as lonely is to which flower?

4. Dunder Mifflin is to Wernham Hogg as Michael Scott is to whom?

5. J and X are to 8 as Q and Z are to 10 as K is to what?

6. The forename of a politician whose unsuccessful campaign to become Prime Minster used the Twitter hashtag #PM4PM is to the surname of an American poet who wrote *The Cantos* as (less formally) which fictional rabbit is to a puppet who appeared in advertisements for PG Tips and ITV Digital?

7. An evergreen coniferous tree which may be followed by the word 'Hill' to form the name of a band is to a city in Flanders which was the centre of three First World War battles as Matthew, Mark, Luke or John is to which composer?

8. Cric, Crac and Croc are to Quebec as who are to the English-speaking world?

This round is out of 8.

WHAT DO THE FOLLOWING HAVE IN COMMON? (NO. 2)

1. An unknown number, the number ten and a kiss?

2. Flay Otters, Fatty Owls and Watery Fowls?

3. Monte, Offen and Schoen?

4. RAS syndrome, Stigler's law of eponymy and sesquipedalianism?

5. *The Vanishing*, *The Ten Commandments*, *Funny Games* and *The Man Who Knew Too Much*?

6. Micael Delaoglou, Mohandas Dewese, David John Harman and Pauline Matthews?

7. A diarist whose grandchildren include Helena Bonham Carter, the winner of the fifth series of *I'm A Celebrity… Get Me Out Of Here*, the youngest British prime minister and the author of *The Castle of Otranto*?

8. Ice, wolves, cards and lies?

This round is out of 8.

TIME FLIES VENN YOU'RE HAVING FUN

What should go in the middle of each Venn diagram? (That is to say, what could fit into both the group on the left and the group on the right?)

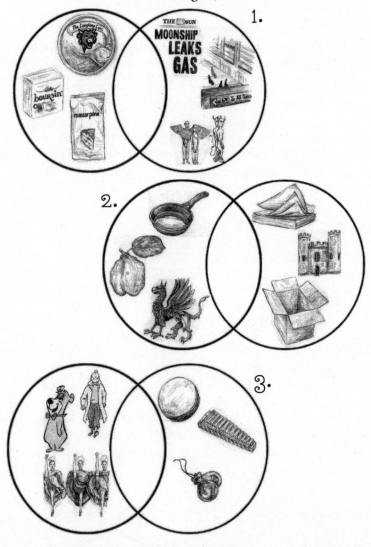

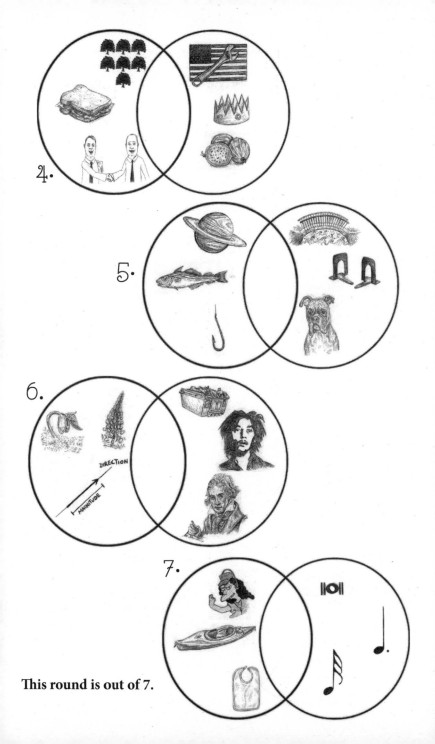

4.

5.

6.

7.

This round is out of 7.

PART FOUR:
POETIC JUSTICE

THE HIDDEN POEM

1. The TV series *Sing Me a Story with Belle* is a spin-off from which Disney film?

2. The punning title of a Ross O'Carroll Kelly novel, in which O'Carroll Kelly has rhinoplasty, parodies the title of a 1997 slasher film starring Jennifer Love Hewitt and Sarah Michelle Gellar. What is the novel called? (Hint: the pun does not include the word 'nose'.)

3. A 2008 survey revealed the advertising slogans that British people are most likely to use in everyday conversation. 'It does exactly what it says on the tin' came third, 'Every little helps' came second, but which slogan associated with a beer came first?

4. '[F]or all their kiddie consciousness, junk-culture arcana and suburban in-jokes, they're in the new tradition — you can dance to them, which counts for plenty when disjunction is your problem,' ran a review of which 1989 rap album, which includes the song 'Me Myself and I'?

5. Which classic children's book, by the author of *Pagan Papers*, features an appearance by the god Pan, whom two of the characters encounter while searching for a lost otter?

6. Watchet harbour boasts a statue of which poem's title character? The poem's author is thought to have been inspired to write it when walking nearby with William and Dorothy Wordsworth.

7. According to John Seabrook's book *The Song Machine: Inside the Hit Factory*, the chorus to which 1998 pop song can be explained by the fact that it was written by two Swedes who were under the impression that 'hit' was American slang for 'call'?

8. If you take a word from each of these answers in order, you can piece together the opening line of a work by which poet?

This round is out of 8.

WORDSEARCH POEM: BIRDS

*Find the names of eighteen birds hidden in this poem (including its title). They may be written forwards or backwards, and may be divided between words and separated by punctuation or line breaks. For example, the words 'over**ook cuc**umber' would yield 'cuckoo'. The name of each bird is at least four letters long. No letter overlaps between more than one bird (so, for instance, if you found 'chaffinch', you couldn't count 'finch' as a separate answer). Have half a point for each answer.**

Ingredients of Impossibility

You who never hear my story

Will quarrel, brawl and blindly sweat

Just to assort a blaze of glory

And bitter, nauseous regret

Into your scant emotional ark

Between archaic long-lost riches,

You venomous wanderers through the dark,

Cudgelling any mite that twitches

Alert, ephemeral, in nether oneness,

Deep, where tenderness lies, sunless.

This round is out of 9.

....

*   On a couple of occasions, teams entrusted with the task of marking each other's papers forgot that each correct answer in the wordsearch poem was worth only half a point. The first time this happened, a team who should rightfully have come second were announced as second from bottom, while the second time I presented the winnings to a team of students, only to snatch them away again once the mistake was discovered. The students took this very graciously. Since then, whenever I have presented a wordsearch poem I have emphasised its scoring system with alarming intensity.

ANAGRAM POEM: FICTIONAL BIRDS

Each line of the following poem (including its title) is an anagram of a fictional bird. The fictional birds are individuals (such as Foghorn Leghorn) rather than types of bird (such as mockingjay). Solve the nine anagrams.

Wow! Doped Cookery!

More toe-hogs

Mock crude cogs

In pliant fact.

Turd who hacked

Hitler, lend teeth

To J. Angus van Gallons in Leith.

Hens sat over me…

Pluck me, Dame Judi D.!

This round is out of 9.

Wordsearch Poem: Capitals

Find the names of eighteen capital cities of countries hidden in this poem (including its title). They may be written forwards or backwards, and may be divided between words and separated by punctuation or line breaks. Accents on letters have been omitted. For example, the words 'a tail is arbitrary' would yield 'Brasília'. No letter overlaps between more than one city. Have half a point for each answer.

An Encounter with a Rare Crop
of Fish that Tell a Vivid Tale

December lingers dreamily,

Its breath enswathed in motion.

A hibernating grey expanse,

That all-demolishing ocean…

A Tsar of ruin with no remorse,

No slouching, no half measures!

A mad libido has swayed its heart

To drag you to its treasures.

Now snatch out from your satchel

Sinking, sinking stones!

Soar up, arise to Brahmin skies

From maledict unknowns.

This round is out of 9.

THE CLERIHEWS OF E.C. BENTLEY

Edmund Clerihew Bentley (1875–1956) invented the clerihew, a poem formed from a pair of couplets summarising the life of a famous person in a humorous and irreverent style. Here are eight of Bentley's clerihews with the subject of each poem left out; you have to guess who it is.

1. Who

Abominated gravy?

He lived in the odium

Of having discovered Sodium.

2. Who

Ate lampreys till he burst?

His unfortunate decease

Simply ruined the Norman peace.

3. Who

Said, 'I am going to dine with some men.

If anybody calls

Say I am designing St. Paul's?'

4. Who

Is a case for legislation ad hoc?

He seems to think nobody minds

His books being all of different kinds.

5.   When they told whom
He didn't know how to cooee,
He replied, 'Perhaps I mayn't,
But I do know how to paint'?

6.   Who,
Among other notable feats,
Drank off a soup tureen,
Full of the true, the blushful Hippocrene?

7.   Who
Wished the Channel could be tunnelled.
He always said it got his goat
To be asked if he had lunched on the boat?

8.   Who,
By a mighty effort of will,
Overcame his natural bonhomie
And wrote *Principles of Political Economy*?

This round is out of 8.

WORDSEARCH POEM: CHEESE

*Find the names of fifteen cheeses hidden in this poem (including its title). They may be written forwards or backwards, and may be divided between words and separated by punctuation or line breaks. For example, the words 'sc**reen a p**hone call' would yield 'paneer'. The name of each cheese is at least four letters long. No letter overlaps between more than one cheese. Where a punctuation mark or diacritical mark occurs in the name of a cheese, it has been missed out. Have half a point for each answer.*

The Tarantula's Trophy: A Poem

Mental leeches, hirelings of Lady El,

Climb, urge, ransack our unmade brains,

'Til tongues – that once with laughter ached – dare tell

Of naught but fearsome Lady El's new chains.

Who but you can stop this hateful fleet?

So curb our sinful foes with your sobriety.

Sharp like a stingray and, like apricot tart, sweet,

Mock them, rend them asunder by your piety!

This round is out of 7½.

ANAGRAM POEM: FICTIONAL EDUCATION

Each line of the following poem (including its title) is an anagram of a fictional school or fictional educational institution. Solve the nine anagrams.

Nits' Sin: Art?

War ghost

Bled a holy host.

Worm's toy earl:

'Hen? Gal? Girl?'

Hen had us lying.

Peter Andre's lime, flying,

Castrated, may feel

Her octopus leg or eel.

This round is out of 9.

THE RHYMESTER'S FURY

Use these definitions to identify each pair of words (for instance, gladiator and radiator) which look like they should rhyme but don't. *Have half a point for each word identified.*

1. A plant whose seed-like fruit is used as a spice and distant

2. Put forward and more self-satisfied than anyone else

3. Extravagant and a word used to describe the tricks employed by the King's enemies in 'God Save the King'

4. A fever, particularly a malarial fever, and a word for a highly infectious disease, which may also mean a calamity sent as divine retribution or a constant source of trouble or annoyance

5. Help and Charles Mingus, Tina Weymouth or Roger Waters, for instance

6. A reduction in price and a nobleman

7. A turban or mitre, for instance, and write a new destination on an envelope

8. A brief and casual romantic or sexual relationship and an agreement to work together

This round is out of 8.

---

* Admittedly, 'gladiator' and 'radiator' do rhyme when pronounced by some residents of Philadelphia.

WORDSEARCH POEM: BONES

*Hidden in the following poem (including its title) are sixteen bones (or groups of bones) of the body. They may be written forwards or backwards, and may be separated by spaces, line breaks or punctuation (for example, 'Te**sla's rat ate m**eat' would hide 'metatarsals'). No letter overlaps between more than one bone. Identify the bones. Each one is at least four letters long. Have half a point for each answer.*

Trevor Versus Rats, Apes and More!

I am Trevor, the conqueror man,

Luscious nature at my command!

I bleed beasts, and I bash them to bran

With my mallet, a pain their souls demand!

A mighty master of jiu-jitsu, I dare

Slap raccoons. With drum effects, trumpet,

I deafen a coypu, bisect a bear

And leave it as full of holes as a crumpet.

So have no nymphal anxieties, reader, no fear!

Be Trevor to the max, ill at ease without strife!

Master numberless wildebeest, apes and reindeer,

Pursue llamas in Mumbai, bite rats in Fife!

This round is out of 8.

COMPLETE THE LIMERICKS

1

In '11, a city did cower

From an earthquake of horrible power

And I'd bet you a tenner

It bent the antenna

Of the red and white…

2

I'd thought that the top room was spare.

My fiancé's mad wife was up there.

That man wanted bigamy!

I feel small as a pygmy.

I'm leaving! Yours truly, …

3

Cheryl's ex, who was once number three,

And a chatty man met up for tea.

But the meeting was bombing:

They had nothing in common

Except the initials…

4

When a spider would bite some poor fella,

They say he'd dance like Cinderella.

But the truth's less peculiar:

A place in Apulia

Gave that fast dance its name: …

5

When I watched *High Noon* on the telly,

The lead actress put fire in my belly,

Though I think I preferred her

In *Dial M for Murder*.

What a huge fan I am of…

6

That courtesan, famous and starry,

Was as fishy as fresh calamari,*

So said bigwigs in France.

She had danced her last dance.

A firing squad shot…

7

The Doors song that I most admire,

If reworded by Spooner, esquire,

Would concern discontent

With my stringed instrument:

Its new title would be…

8

My mother said, 'Why'd you repeal

The Corn Laws? And when people squeal,

"Help those starving Irish!"

You simply say, "Why rush?"'

She'd confused me with Sir…

This round is out of 8.

....

*   I realise that 'as cephalopodic as fresh calamari' would be more taxonomically
accurate, but I opted for 'fishy' for the sake of both scansion and sense. Apologies to
offended pedants.

WORDSEARCH POEM: MYTHICAL CREATURES

*Find the names of sixteen mythical creatures hidden in this poem. They may be written forwards or backwards and may be separated by spaces, punctuation or line breaks (for instance, 'his **usage** **p**lummeted' would reveal 'Pegasus'). No letter overlaps between more than one creature. The answers may be types of creature (such as 'unicorn') or specific creatures (such as Medusa). Each creature is at least four letters long, and each one is worth half a point.*

Blind Lemon Jefferson

Blind Lemon Jefferson traces his descent

Aurally, in the dewy vernacular,

As a squat child of a councillor takes down his tent,

Unsure Brecht would condone an act so unspectacular.

Lemon glorifies the romantic or even foolhardy.

He's wrapped in his turban, sheepish as a wallflower.

Ewer of wallflowers he is, steady and sturdy,

His tongue free from the fiery taste of power.

As distant as Syria, Fallujah, Yemen

Is the bluesman's retrogressive moan:

'I'd rather go blind… I'd rather go Lemon.'

While passers-by chant, 'One-nil!', merging into a drone.

This round is out of 8.

MORE ELOQUENCE THAN YOU COULD SHAKE A SPEAR AT

These cartoons illustrate seven well-known Shakespeare quotations, as they might appear in the imagination of someone who had heard them out of context and misunderstood their meaning. Identify the quotations.

1. (*HAMLET*, 6 WORDS)

2. (*MACBETH*, 3 WORDS)

3. (*ROMEO AND JULIET*, 5 WORDS)

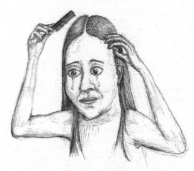

4. (HENRY IV PART 2, 8 WORDS)

5. (ROMEO AND JULIET, 6 WORDS)

6. (ANTONY AND CLEOPATRA, 2 WORDS)

7. (JULIUS CAESAR, 9 WORDS)

This round
is out of 7.

COMPLETE THE LIMERICKS, ANOTHER WAY

*The three words that should fill in each limerick's trio of blank spaces are anagrams of each other. Have a point for each limerick correctly completed, or half a point for getting two out of three words.**

1.

The work of three _____ from _____

Depicts the Queen clad as a jester.

Their preparatory sketches

All show how she _____

With horror at how they have dressed her.

2.

There was a young man from _____

Whom _____ games drove up the wall.

To be far from *QI*,

He flew through the sky

In a _____ he'd named 'Toksvig's Downfall'.

3.

There was a young lady from _____

Who _____ a small cat in her corset.

In her life, she reported,

Each problem was _____:

To the cat she would always outsource it.

....

*   The format of this puzzle was inspired by a puzzle from *The GCHQ Puzzle Book*, where five blank spaces in a limerick had to be filled by words that formed a 5 x 5 square where the same answers can fit both horizontally and vertically. Also, apologies if some of the rhymes (such as 'Dorking' and 'walking') do not rhyme in your accent.

4.

It took me ten years to invent it:

A robot that _____ me – and meant it!

But it fell in a hole

And _____ seized my soul –

All that I've _____ to… prevented!

5.

All _____ living in Hawes

Were suffering from _____and sores

Except one _____

Who ate kale and polenta

While the others ate deep-fried cats' paws.

6.

Three DVD _____ from Dorking

(Whose _____ had stopped them from walking)

Yelled, 'Hey there, film scholars!

Buy *A Fistful of Dollars*!

Its hero, who's _____, is corking!'

7.

Many's the _____ he cried

When the monster in _____ died.

He screeched, 'Oh, how grim!'

'Grim!' I _____ him

And that's why he made me his bride.

8.

At Christmas, I light up the fires

And eagerly _____ to choirs.

As they sing '_____ Night',

Which fills me with delight,

I wind _____ round telegraph wires.

This round is out of 8.

Wordsearch Poem: Cars

*Find the names of sixteen brands of car hidden in the following poem (including its title). They may be written forwards or backwards, divided between words or between lines (for example, 'Mage**ll**an **drove r**eindeer' would reveal 'Land Rover'). No letter overlaps between more than one car. Each car brand has at least four letters, and each is worth half a point.*

When Bonfires Supersede Crematoria:
A Poem (or a Flame?)

Did Pavlov love his dog? Did he give his dog a bone

Or tickle her soft paunch, in shrill falsetto call,

'I'd ache without you, Vita, if you left me all alone!

I'd drink hydrofluoric acid, I'd drink nauseating gall!'

Or did he let his needlepoint transport him into stupors,

Chew and crunch on dainty treats, his Vita's very own?

Did he with dishonour, abuse and bile diminish his dear trooper?

What a fiendish individual to owe a dog a bone!

This round is out of 8.

ANAGRAM POEM: WOMEN WHO CHANGED THE WORLD

Each line of the following poem (including its title) is an anagram of one of the Independent's *'100 women who changed the world'. Solve the nine anagrams.*

Sister: A Poem

Flirting spy dudes,

Male supermen, think

Nine TV wives – wooed

By holiest drink

(A quince julep, red

As molten tin, girl!) –

Dive, blitz ahead,

Sail, canoe, curl!

This round is out of 9.

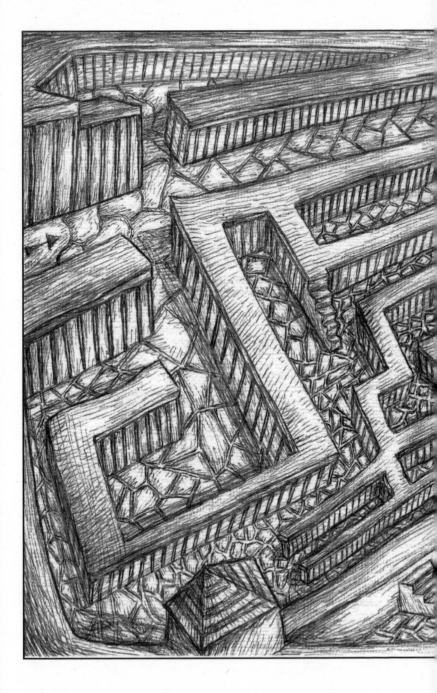

PART FIVE:
WORDPLAY

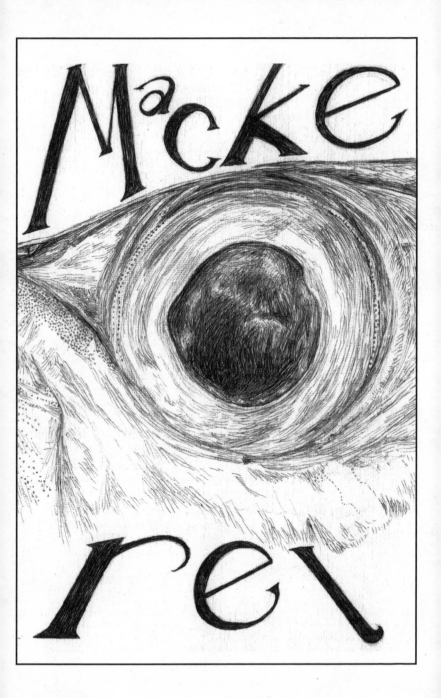

HOLY MACKEREL!*

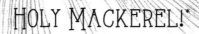

1. Which chemical element has the shortest name, and is also the only one not to contain any letters of the word 'mackerel'?

2. Which of the seven traditional colours of the rainbow is the only one not to contain any letters of the word 'mackerel'?

3. Which is the only Northern Irish county to contain none of the letters of the word 'mackerel' (that is, if you exclude the word 'County' at the beginning)?

4. Which Old Testament book has the shortest name, as well as being the only one in the King James Bible** not to contain any of the letters of the word 'mackerel'?

....

*   This round was inspired by a friend informing me that there is only one London Underground station which contains none of the letters of the word 'mackerel' (though this would not be so if the first word of the station's name were written in its full form). The name of the station in question will be revealed along with the answers. The phrase 'Holy mackerel!' is thought originally to have been a euphemism for 'Holy Mary!'.

** In some other versions Song of Solomon is known by the non-mackerelly alias Song of Songs.

5. Apart from 'Go!', which is the only space on a standard London *Monopoly* board that contains no letters of the word 'mackerel'?

6. What, described by one critic as 'a musical film that bears such a basic resemblance to *My Fair Lady* that the authors may want to sue themselves', became in 1958 the first sound film to win the Best Picture Oscar while also containing no letters of the word 'mackerel'? And, for a bonus point, what was the first film – as well as the only fully silent film – to win the Best Picture Oscar, which also contained no letters of the word 'mackerel'?

7. Which two African nations, both of which are coastal countries north of the Equator, share no letters with the word 'mackerel'? (Have a point for each.)

8. Which is the only US state to share no letters with the word 'mackerel'?

This round is out of 10.

2 BECOME 1 (NO. 1)

Here are pairs of definitions of eight words. In each case the first definition treats the word as if it had been divided into two words. For example, 'the fury of a sheltered inlet and the reporting of an event on the news' would be 'cove rage/coverage'. 'The pain of a metal container and flair' would be 'pan ache/panache'. Identify the pairs of words.

1. A conservative formed from molten rock and a washroom

2. The body of traditional knowledge surrounding a small mythological creature and beseech

3. A crop grown on an Italian island and a star sign

4. A limit on the amount of light fabric you're allowed to have and a deep cut

5. A spasmodic movement found in a European capital and amorous

6. Nothing but a cold brittle substance and fairness

7. Last-minute recovery and in a way that relates to an unusual and creative type of thinking.

8. A building material made from you and me and a declaration

This round is out of 8.

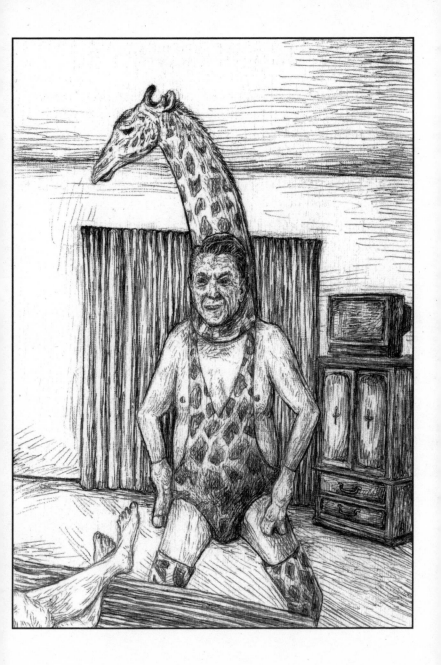

FILL IN THE BLANKS

Fill in the blanks to form coherent (though occasionally rather surreal) sentences. In each sentence, the two blank spaces must be filled by the same sequence of letters, though the letters of at least one in each pair will be separated by at least one space; each set of letters in the pair may also be punctuated differently. For instance, in the sentence, 'Her fiancé left her soon after proposing when he discovered she had sold _____ to buy some pickled _____', the first blank should be filled by 'her ring' and the second with 'herring'. Have half a point for each blank space correctly filled.

1. I had difficulty _____ why she always communicated with me using such a _____ pigeon that it could barely fly.

2. He used his skill in _____ to build a wooden barrier in the fish pond, denying the _____ to a section he had reserved for trout.

3. Ronald Reagan, sensing that a certain _____ had crept into his marriage, began disguising himself as various hoofed mammals in the bedroom, and it soon became clear that it was the _____ liked best.

4. When my friends grow sick, I feed them fruit bat soup
   (which only makes _____

   bread and fermented sardines, and read them

   _____ by Geoffrey Chaucer.

5. The president of the literature society (who considered works
   without Christian allegory to be _____

   the members' attention to C.S. Lewis's *The Magician's Nephew*,

   and began to speak animatedly about the relationship between

   Digory and his _____.

6. Instead of bandaging the director of *Wings of
   Desire*'s wound, I decided to take a stroll through

   _____ Common, as a consequence of

   which _____.

7. I was so moved by *Art of the Early 20th Century* magazine's
   decision to make Paul _____ cover

   star that I reached for a box of _____.

8. The horse trainer finally decided to take Dr.

   _____ advice, 'You wanna make noise,

   make noise' and abandoned _____ for

   a more gangsta lifestyle.

This round is out of 8.

AD'D THE ANIMAL

Guess each pair of words from their definitions. The pairs of words are spelt identically except for the addition of the name of an animal inserted somewhere inside, or at either end of, the second word. For instance, 'a filled pastry and a marauder' would give you 'pie' and 'pirate'. Have half a point for each word.

1. Agreed and elaborate or difficult

2. Suffer distress and make an enemy of

3. A soft cheese and for a short stretch of time

4. Fell and a part of a plant used to symbolise desolation or an awkward silence

5. Dishonest statements and events at which winners are selected at random from among ticketholders

6. Beseeched and having limbs that curve outwards

7. A male cat and either a place name or any name derived from a place name

8. A component and a defensive wall in a fortification (There are two possible answers to this, both of which use the same first word. Have one and a half points if you get them both.)

This round is out of 8½.

ANAGRAMS PLUS ONE (NO. 1)

Each answer from 2 to 8 is an anagram of the previous answer but with one extra letter added.

1. Which word is shared in the titles of a 1992 film about competing real estate agents and a BBC series from the early 2000s set in the Scottish Highlands?

2. What name is shared by an American spin-off TV series, a London tube station and songs by Aerosmith and Madonna?

3. Which film director once said, 'Making a martial arts film in English to me is the same as John Wayne speaking Chinese in a western'?

4. Which soul singer became a Baptist minister and turned his attentions to gospel music, the supposed catalyst for this conversion being a 1974 incident in which his girlfriend poured scalding hot grits over him before killing herself with his gun?

5. Zod, Grievous, Yen and Titus Andronicus are all fictional what?

6. Bellatrix and Rudolphus, a villainous married couple in the *Harry Potter* books, have what surname?

干脆把培根放在小饼上,就走咯!
我们要争分夺秒,伙计们!

7. 'Science created him. Now Chuck Norris must destroy him' is the tagline to which 1982 film, in which Norris plays the sheriff of a Texas town who is pitted against a mute serial killer with a superhuman ability to self-heal?

8. According to *The Sunday Telegraph*, who, in his memoir *Toast: The Story of a Boy's Hunger*, displays '[a] talent for prose as simple and pleasurable as his recipes'?

This round is out of 8.

PALINDROME (NO. 1)*

The answers to this round collectively form a palindrome (if spaces and punctuation are disregarded) but none of the answers individually is a palindrome. A palindrome is a word or phrase which reads the same forwards and backwards.

1. Hawaii is one of only two US states to have a double vowel in its name. Which is the other? (For clarity, I'm talking about two of the same vowel next to one another, so Ohio, for example, wouldn't count.)

2. Which treacle-like substance, derived from boiling down juice from sugar cane, was the most popular sweetener in the USA before refined sugar became affordable?

3. The names of three countries recognised by the UN, all of which are Arab states, start with a letter that no other country begins with. Two of them are Yemen and Qatar; which is the third?**

4. Which first name is shared by the protagonist of *The Vampire Diaries*, a former British number-one tennis player who died in 2014 and the wife of Romanian dictator Nicolae Ceaușescu?

5. Which character has been portrayed by Charlton Heston and Burt Lancaster, as well as in 2014 by Christian Bale, who controversially described him as 'likely schizophrenic and was one of the most barbaric individuals that I ever read about in my life'?

....

* I have a long-standing fondness for palindromes. I wrote palindromic poems in my student days, and it was a source of great delight to me when some sliver of surreal coherence arose from my workings (one such effort ran, 'Oho!/Pull a lid off a demon,/Gasping an "alas"./An osteopath-girl lay/As nil, a nerd, a warning./Inebriate Lara,/Let air, benign in raw adrenalin,/Say, "All right"./A poet: "So nasal a nag nips a gnome!"/Daffodil, all up, oho!').

** At the time of writing, Western Sahara has not been recognised by the UN as an independent country and as such does not count as a valid answer.

6. Which first-century woman was the title character of both an Oscar Wilde play and a Richard Strauss opera?

7. Which German city is also the German word for food?

8. Which word can precede 'ball', 'curtains', 'result' and 'work' to make four common words and phrases?

This round is out of 8.

IT ALL ADDS UP: TELEVISION

*Use the following visual clues – **which always relate to sounds rather than spellings** – to assemble the titles of seven TV programmes. When a clue, or a bracketed set of clues, is followed by a **minus sign**, it indicates that the sounds corresponding to the clue or bracketed set of clues immediately after the minus sign must be removed and replaced with the clue or bracketed set of clues immediately after the **plus sign**. The role of the comma is simply to emphasise that it does not form a bracketed set with another clue. For example, if a picture representing an **epigram** were followed by a **minus sign**, a picture representing a **gram**, a **plus sign** and a picture representing someone called **Quinn**, this would give you the title of the short-lived game show* Epic Win.

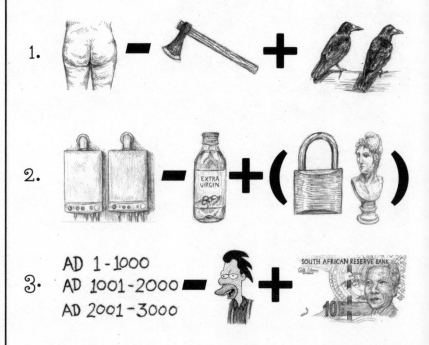

1.

2.

3.

AD 1 - 1000
AD 1001 - 2000
AD 2001 - 3000

EXTRA VIRGIN

SOUTH AFRICAN RESERVE BANK
10

ANAGRAMS: PERSONAL ADS

Each line of the following personal ads is an anagram of the title of a romantic comedy. The number to the left of each anagram indicates the year that that film came out. Solve the nine anagrams.

(2012)   ● **Love??** Slinky Paris goblin,

(1989)   a sly hyena, WLTM 'Herr

(1940)   Hip-hop Hitler'… a sly date?

(1986)   ● **Nippy** knitter

(1998)   needs gig nerd with

(1960)   rampant teeth.

(1997)   ● **Dirty Deb** finds new gems?

(2008)   Shall I trash ragtag men for

(1998)   bigamy, threesome or 'nut hats'?

This round is out of 9.

CRAWL INSIDE MY IDIOM ATTIC

This round focuses on shared words in idiomatic phrases.

1. What, according to separate idioms, is disturbed by those who do not get to the point as well as housing creatures half as valuable as those in captivity?

2. What, according to separate idioms, bears comparison with an industrious person while having splendid joints?

3. What, according to separate idioms, can be an important personage when it is of great size, while having nothing in common with the skeletal remains of plankton?

4. According to separate idioms, a meal in which participants share the cost, a stern critic and the lack of inhibitions associated with intoxication share which nationality?

5. Which seven-letter word, according to two separate idioms, might bear comparison with an eager person and be separated by a competent person?

6. Which seven-letter word, according to two separate idioms, is either the most basic starting point or a point that must be reached in order to have made satisfactory progress?

7. Which five-letter word, according to separate idioms, is it legitimate to be above and all-inclusive to be across?

8. What, according to separate idioms, may suffer from fatal inquisitiveness or seize the fleshy organ of a silent person?

This round is out of 8.

ALPHABETICAL ANTICS (NO. 1)

The answers to this round collectively contain every letter of the alphabet once and only once.

1. Meanings of which word include a macho young man, a derogatory term for a Scotsman and a person who plays recorded music for an audience?

2. The actor and former wrestler Lawrence Tureaud is better known by what name?

3. Those in the RAF who fought in the Battle of Britain are often described as the what, a reference to a quotation from Winston Churchill as well as the St Crispin's Day speech from Shakespeare's *Henry V*?

4. Boxers Vitali and Wladimir Klitschko and Queen guitarist Brian May are all entitled to use which three-letter abbreviation after their names?

5. What name is shared by an annual music festival, an anarchist comic book character and Thomas Pynchon's first novel?

6. Which big cat is also the name of a product known in many countries as Axe?

7. What is the highest-scoring four-letter *Scrabble* word that can be played using a standard set of *Scrabble* tiles (ignoring bonus squares)?

8. Which four-letter word can mean 'containers', 'plenty' and 'a child's way of laying claim to something'?

This round is out of 8.

GOGGLEBOX JIGSAW

Each answer can be considered a piece of a jigsaw: the order that the answers come in must be rearranged and spaces inserted in the appropriate places (though the order of letters of each individual answer will stay the same). Once a missing 'piece' is inserted into the jigsaw, it will then spell out the name of a TV programme.

1. Which word, which usually has negative connotations, has a more positive meaning in hip-hop slang, and is found in this sense in the title of the Beastie Boys' first album, where it is preceded by the words 'License to'?

2. Which 2008 biographical film takes its title from the middle initial of its subject and has the tagline 'A life misunderestimated'?

3. The titles of Billie Piper's debut single and a sequel to *Dumb and Dumber* which was released 20 years after the first film both end with which word?

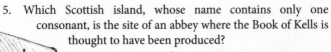

4. Which educational children's TV programme, which aired from 1966–1981, began with the presenters each raising one hand and announcing the title, a reference to the fact that the title can also be a stereotypical Native American greeting?

5. Which Scottish island, whose name contains only one consonant, is the site of an abbey where the Book of Kells is thought to have been produced?

6. Meanings of which word include 'piece of metal or wood', 'ray of light' and 'smile joyfully'?

7. Which word meaning 'anger' can mean 'awful' if the letter 'd' is placed in front of it and 'marsh' if the letter 'm' is placed in front of it?

8. Which creatures form the missing part of the jigsaw, and which TV show is formed when the jigsaw is complete (for half a point each)?

This round is out of 8.

WORDS OF CHARACTER

A round on words derived from the names of fictional characters.

1. Which hyphenated word, taken from the name of a character in a 1999 comedy sequel, is defined by Oxford Dictionaries as '[a] person closely resembling a smaller or younger version of another'?

2. Which word for a short publication without binding or hard covers is derived from the title character of a twelfth-century Latin poem which was widely copied and distributed? The character's name is derived from the Greek for 'loved by all'.

3. Which American word for a nerd or egghead is taken from the name of a character in the animated series *Felix the Cat*?

4. The modern sense of which word, meaning an uninformed or foolish person, comes from the title character of a 1615 Latin-language play by George Ruggle? The word was also once used in a legal context, with the grand jury having the option to write it on a bill to indicate that they found the prosecution's evidence insufficient.

5. Which American portmanteau word meaning a very intelligent person was previously used as the name of a super-intelligent villain in the *Superman* comics?

6. Which phrase meaning an annoyingly virtuous person was popularised by a children's story attributed to Oliver Goldsmith? It becomes the nickname of the impoverished title character after a rich gentleman gives her footwear.

7.   Which term for a photographer is taken from the name of a character in Federico Fellini's film *La Dolce Vita*?

8.   Which word for a seducer of women was popularised by the name of a character in Nicholas Rowe's 1703 play *The Fair Penitent*? A character of the same name had appeared in *Don Quixote*, where he was asked by his friend Anselmo to attempt to seduce his wife in order to test her fidelity.*

This round is out of 8.

---

*   This plan, perhaps inevitably, backfired on Anselmo.

PALINDROME (NO. 2)

The answers to this round collectively form a palindrome (if spaces and punctuation are disregarded) but none of the answers individually is a palindrome.

1. Which Hebridean island, if you add one letter before and one letter after its final letter, becomes a group of Greek islands?

2. The name of which priestess in Greek mythology is also the title of songs by Mariah Carey and Enrique Iglesias?

3. Nick Cave drafted the script for a never-made sequel to which 2000 film? Cave's draft featured gods threatened by the popularity of monotheism resurrecting the main character from the dead and sending him back in time with the aim of killing Jesus Christ. The main character then ends up becoming immortal and fighting in many of history's major wars.

4. Which band, whose songs include 'Rosanna' and 'Africa', shares its name with Dorothy's dog in *The Wizard of Oz*?

5. Which word, denoting a way of walking or running, is also a derogatory term for someone who sympathises with, or is suspected of sympathising with, the ideology of a certain Marxist thinker?

6. Which word is shared in the names of an organisation which has used the slogan, 'We believe in life before death', an electronic amplifier worn in the ear and a supergroup who released a chart-topping charity single in 1984?

7. Who shared a Harvard University room with Tommy Lee Jones and went on to share a Nobel Prize with the Intergovernmental Panel on Climate Change?

8. Which Asian capital city houses a mausoleum containing the embalmed body of the country's former president, despite that president having stated in his will that he wanted to be cremated?

This round is out of 8.

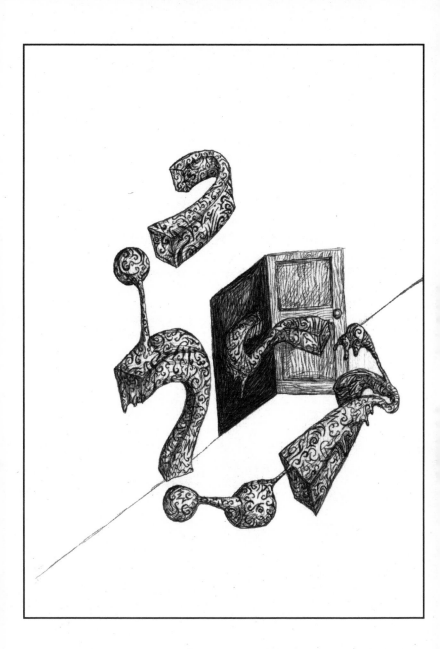

BUILD YOUR OWN WORDSEARCH

1. Which insulting term for a fool or bungler is the nickname conferred by Archie Bunker on his son-in-law in the sitcom *All in the Family* as well as the nickname of an American cook, the author of a book of the same name subtitled *The Science of Great Barbecue and Grilling*?

2. Which word originally meant 'divinely conferred gift or power' but is now more commonly used to mean 'compelling attractiveness or charm'? It is the first name of an actress who appeared in *Buffy the Vampire Slayer* and its spin-off *Angel*.

3. Which word is defined by Merriam-Webster as 'a light or humorous verse form of five chiefly anapestic verses of which lines 1, 2, and 5 are of three feet and lines 3 and 4 are of two feet with a rhyme scheme of *aabba*'?

4. Which two-word term for a genre of music did Iggy Pop claim was 'used by dilettantes and heartless manipulators, about music that takes up the energies, and the bodies, and the hearts and the souls and the time and the minds, of young men, who give what they have to it, and give everything they have to it. And it's a – it's a term that's based on contempt'? He carried on to say, 'I don't know Johnny Rotten, but I'm sure, I'm sure he puts as much blood and sweat into what he does as Sigmund Freud did.'

5. A phrase meaning 'the majority bring their vehicles to a halt' is a spoonerism of which word, meaning something which may be applied to an envelope?

6. Which adverb, meaning 'in a manner characteristic of a group which may share ancestors and customs', is an anagram of the name of the central character in Edith Wharton's *The House of Mirth*?

7. If you take the surname of a German engineer often credited with producing the world's first practical automobile and follow it with the symbols for yttrium, lithium and carbon, this spells out which word, an adjective used in chemistry to mean 'relating to a particular radical or its derivatives'?

8. The Jesuit missionary Jean de Brébeuf is thought to have been the first to use which term to denote a sport he witnessed played among the Huron in what is now Ontario? It was a medal sport in the 1904 and 1908 Olympics.

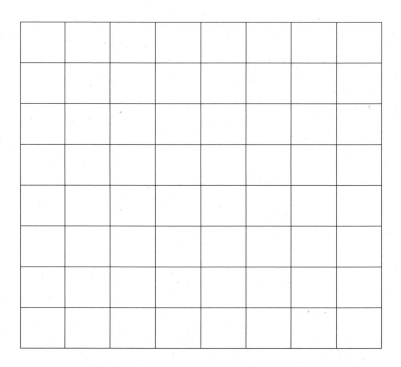

*If the eight answers in this round are inserted horizontally into the grid, six names – which have something in common with (but do not include) one of this round's answers – can be found. They may be found forwards or backwards, horizontally, vertically or diagonally. Identify the six hidden names, for **half a point each**.*

This round is out of 11.

ALPHABETICAL ANTICS (NO. 2)

The answers to this round collectively contain every letter of the alphabet once and only once.

1. Which four-letter word denotes a plant which has blue flowers and produces linseed?

2. Which word, used in the King James Bible to mean 'alive', can also mean sensitive flesh under the fingernails, which someone can idiomatically be cut to if they are emotionally hurt?

3. By what name was John Cleese's character credited in *The World Is Not Enough*, which referred to the fact that he was Q's assistant?

4. Which 2015 film was reviewed by the *Telegraph* under the headline 'Miss Moneypenny unleashed'?

5. Which two-letter abbreviation is the profession of a saviour in a song by Indeep?

6. What was an early pen name of Charles Dickens, as well as being the nickname of a musician who released the album *Silk Degrees*?

7. About which programme, which broadcast its last episode in 2010, did a *Guardian* journalist reminisce, 'Where else could Penny Smith have been the newscaster? Or someone like Fiona Phillips – who once comforted Gerry and Kate McCann by pointing out, "There are light moments, though. You've acquired this odd celebrity status" – been one of the main anchors?'

8. What is the first word of the title of a song first released by Percy Sledge which includes the lyric 'If she's bad he can't see it/She can do no wrong', as well as the first word of the title of a Beatles song which includes the lyric 'Doing the garden, digging the weeds/Who could ask for more'?

This round is out of 8.

2 BECOME 1 (NO. 2)

Here are pairs of definitions of eight words, with the first definition treating it as if it were two words. For example, 'the fury of a sheltered inlet and the reporting of an event on the news' would be 'cove rage/coverage.' Identify the pairs of words.

1. South American ancestry and furious

2. A place for a burrowing animal to stop and harassment

3. A dance music-inspired scowl and fade

4. Iron oxide that has formed upon tiny water droplets and suspicion

5. The most basic recipe imaginable for cooked chicken and a derogatory term for someone who doesn't recognise the God of the Bible

6. The co-writer of 'Do They Know It's Christmas?' standing in plain sight and a piece of music played at the beginning of an opera

7. Waste matter excreted by a fruit and a statuette

8. Boxes for large mammals to be stored and the so-called father of Western medicine

This round is out of 8.

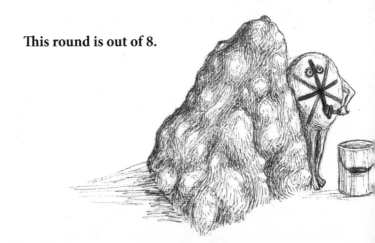

WORDS WITH WOMEN

Guess the two words from their definitions. The words are spelt identically except for the insertion of a woman's name into the beginning, middle or end of the second word. For instance, 'Greatest in amount and driver' gives 'most' and 'motorist'.

1. A support or stage of a journey and looking lasciviously

2. A word whose meanings include counter, forbid and except and daub all over or defile

3. Remove and Ashton Eaton or Daley Thompson, for instance

4. Adhere and climbing using both hands and feet

5. A drunkard and a person who performs unaccompanied

6. Santa's helpers are subordinate Clauses, for instance, and John Bunyan or Oliver Cromwell, for instance

7. Sob and imitation

8. Having lost brightness and (literally) having an oversized skull or (figuratively) idiotic

This round is out of 8.

*Here are some fragments of
sentences, which can be rendered
complete and accurate if the same word,
phrase or name is placed at both ends.*

1. …was formerly the capital of French Somaliland and is now the capital of…

2. …Gallagher was named after his father's hero John…

3. …Baldwin kept above his writing desk a picture of one of his greatest influences: Henry…

4. …is a common invitation to partake of what's available, though if you do so instinctively without being able to muster up any restraint, it may be said of you that you can't…

5. …Miller's retelling of the Battle of Thermopylae was adapted into a film featuring Michael Fassbender, star of the 2014 film…

6. …was the first wife of the twentieth-century English author, satirist and critic…

7. …is the middle name of electronic musician Richard Hall, who took his stage name in honour of his distant relative Herman…

8. …, who painted a work which in 2013 broke the record for the highest price paid for a painting at auction, is thought to have been a descendant of the half-brother of the philosopher and scientist…

This round is out of 8.

PALINDROME (NO. 3)

The answers to this round collectively form a palindrome (if spaces and punctuation are disregarded) but none of the answers individually is a palindrome.

1. Which film, a tale of lust and murder set in a renowned tourist spot, was advertised with the tagline 'A raging torrent of emotion that even nature can't control'?

2. Which seventeenth-century science fiction author was also the subject of a play by Edmond Rostand, which presented a fictionalised version of the novelist's love life?

3. Which area of London, which shares its name with districts of New York City and Hong Kong, is thought to derive its name from an old English hunting cry?

4. Which word meaning 'alarm' can mean 'be interested' if the first letter is removed or 'a residual mark' if the last letter is removed?

5. Which five-letter word denotes a bird similar to a loon? If the second letter of the word is replaced by an 'l', it means 'a plot of land belonging to a parish church'.

6. Which six-letter word is defined as 'a gift given for sacred use'?

7. Which word is shared in the titles of the opening track of the Beatles album *Rubber Soul*, a single from Tracy Chapman's debut album which Chapman described as 'about a relationship that doesn't work out because it's starting from the wrong place' and a 2000 film featuring Seann William Scott described by Common Sense Media as 'a sloppy, unappealing comedy that falls somewhere between Cheech & Chong and Bill & Ted'?

8. Which word occurs at the end of the titles of a western starring Marlene Dietrich and Jimmy Stewart, an Australian parody of the band ABBA and a Britney Spears song, the video for which depicts Spears on Mars addressing an astronaut who has fallen in love with her?

This round is out of 8.

ANAGRAMS PLUS ONE (NO. 2)

Each answer from 2–8 is an anagram of the previous answer but with one extra letter added.

1. Meanings of which word include melody, distinctive quality, broadcast and ventilate?

2. A *Guardian* article in 2012 reported that streets in which country had begun to resemble a 'kidney eBay' owing to the popularity of selling one's kidneys (particularly among poorer residents in their twenties)?

3. Which Scottish town, about 15 miles from Inverness, is renowned for its golf courses and shares its name with the surname of a couple who founded a bakery known for its oatcakes?

4. Which country is bordered to the South by Archenland and to the North by Ettinsmoor and has its seat of government at Cair Paravel?

5. Raymond Babbitt is the title character of which 1988 film?

6. Which word originally meant an official or civil servant before coming to denote a language and a fruit?

7. Which former quarterback for the Miami Dolphins becomes a country if the first letter of his first name is replaced by another letter?

8. Which two-word term for a woman who plays leading roles in an opera company can also mean someone self-important, temperamental and demanding?

This round is out of 8.

In this round, I've written a synopsis of what I imagine various films to have been like if one word of their titles had been spelt backwards. For instance, 'This 2009 satire of Anglo-American politics is set in a swimming bath,' would lead you to In the Pool *(the film itself being* In the Loop*).*

1. This *film noir* stars Humphrey Bogart as private detective Philip Marlowe, a man whose hardboiled demeanour is compromised by the fact that he is constantly slipping on enormous banana skins.

2. This series of fantasy romance films follows characters' struggles as they attempt to operate bulky cooking ranges in the gloom.

3. Jim Carrey's character begins this 1997 film by making an announcement that a train has been delayed owing to leaves on the line. However, he knows full well that the real reason for the train's delay was signal failure.

4. A divorcee prepares to fight an intense legal battle as he faces losing custody of his son not to his estranged ex-wife – or even to a living creature – but to a series of spoken words.

5. Jimmy Stewart and Henry Fonda are among the all-star cast of this epic, which, despite the backdrop of such events as the Gold Rush and the American Civil War, is revealed in fact to be set in the present day.

6. Two rival booksellers, unaware of each other's real identity, share romantic messages. However, instead of using the Internet to communicate, they decide to scrawl their messages onto the lead singer of Oasis and then send him to each other.

7. This sports film features a group of prisoners taking on their guards in a brutal contest to build the most extensive cart.

8. In this thriller it is revealed that a double agent has sabotaged the needlework of the British secret service, which forces them to start work again on making dolls of people with three different professions.

This round is out of 8.

HIDDEN LANDS

Each question has two answers. By piecing together the final letters of the first answer and the first letters of the second, you can make the names of eight countries. Identify the countries (you don't need to name either of the answers that make it up). For example, 'A comic book detective portrayed by Warren Beatty and a former state ruled over by Frederick the Great' would give you 'Dick Tracy/Prussia' – hence, 'Cyprus'.

1. Small Italian dumplings often made with potato and the city in which Richard III is buried

2. According to the Bible, a wise and wealthy king who ordered the building of the First Temple in Jerusalem and a Philistine killed by this king's father

3. A soft drink which, according to one advertising slogan, is 'made in Scotland from girders', and a Canadian musician whose albums include *Harvest*

4. A disease resulting from thiamine deficiency and the word that completes Neil Patrick Harris's comment at the 2015 Oscars after *Citizenfour* won best documentary: 'Edward Snowden couldn't be here for some...'

5. A weapon which, according to the tagline of a film which bears its name, was 'Forged by a god, foretold by a wizard, found by a king' and a word used to denote that a boxer has been recognised as the champion in their weight category by all of the sport's main governing bodies

6. A David Bowie song which begins 'You've got your mother in a whirl/She's not sure if you're a boy or a girl' and a Coldplay album which includes the songs 'Clocks' and 'The Scientist'

7. A character honoured with a statue in Crystal City, Texas, the so-called 'spinach capital of the world', and a character in *The Odyssey* whose name can be used to mean a trusted and experienced adviser

8. A Beatles song which begins with part of the French national anthem and ends with a snippet of 'She Loves You' and a 1953 film noir with Marilyn Monroe and Joseph Cotten

This round is out of 8.

REBUS CROSSWORD

In this two-part puzzle, each set of images in boxes, when read aloud in the direction indicated by the arrow, will provide the answer to its numbered clue. Each image relates to the pronunciation of a syllable or pair of syllables within the answer (for instance, images of a bar, some brass, a rugby player scoring a try and some sand would combine to form the answer 'Barbra Streisand'). Any image which appears in two answers will be pronounced identically in both answers (but not necessarily spelt identically in both answers). However, the images which must fill spaces 'a'–'h' are missing. The missing images can be found in Part Two, and you must decide which box each image should fit into to provide the appropriate answers to the written clues.

PTO.

PART 1

What are the answers to the written clues?

1. Detect using sound waves

2. Steal

3. Item of bedding

4. The art of making sweet-smelling substances

5. Pierce

6. British sitcom

7. Pipeline discharging wastewater into the sea

8. Cloth

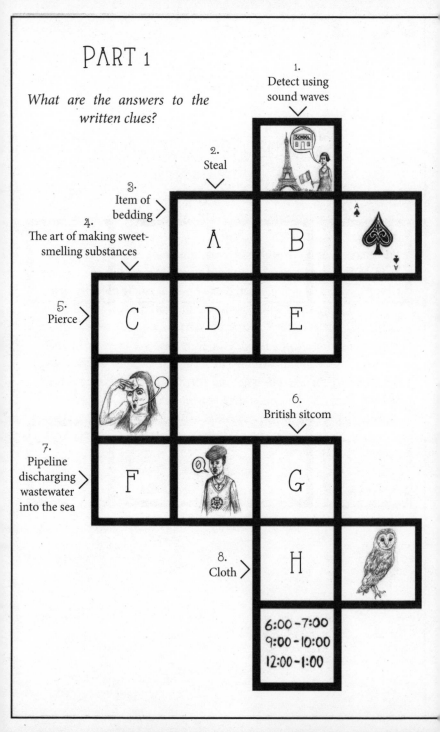

PART 2

In which square of the 'crossword' in Part One does each image belong?

1

2

3

4

5

6

7

8

This round is out of 16.

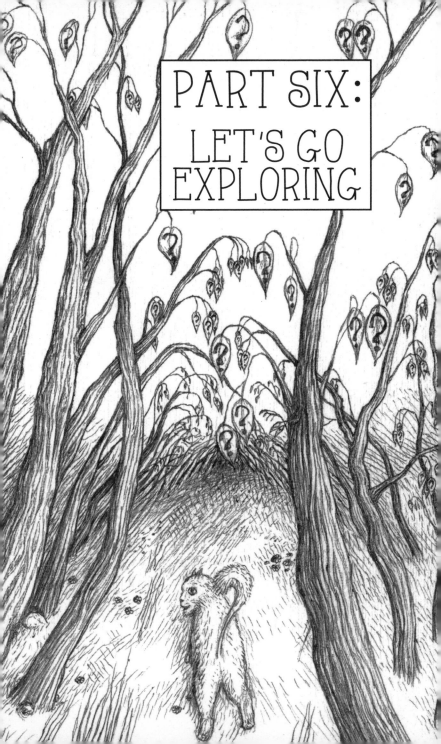

PART SIX:

LET'S GO
EXPLORING

DISCO ISLAND DES

This round traces the adventures of a man called Des, who is shipwrecked and finds himself on Disco Island.

1. At first Des is confused by the inhabitants' 70s clothing and the fact that they are all dancing which dance, which shares its name with a BBC series about con artists?

2. 'We are slaves to disco!' sings one inhabitant of the island. 'What a wonderful word disco is! If you insert it into a word meaning "daydreams", you get a word meaning "instances of finding again".' Which two words is the inhabitant thinking of? (Have half a point for each.)

3. Des decides to make his way to the capital of Disco Island. Its name, which is also the name of a disco hit, can be formed from the first three letters of the capital of Tuvalu, the first two letters of a city which was Japan's capital for over a millennium and the last four letters of the capital of Sierra Leone. What is it called?

4. The capital of Disco Island is guarded by Gloria Gaynor, who is dressed as a Sphinx and warns Des that if he fails to answer her riddle she will eat him. She sings, 'Spelt out so very clear/Which disco group appear/When a musician from Korea/Is subtracted from a seer?'

5. As soon as Des enters the capital's gates, he encounters a musician who appeared in the film *The Wiz*. She demands that he don the flared trousers which make up the city's official dress code, but he insults her by pointing out that her first initial and surname spell out a word meaning 'rubbish', and she runs away. Who is the musician?

6. Exasperated by the capital's incessant boogie, Des takes the Love Train to a secluded forest on the other side of the island. There he meets a tribe who spend their days moving a single seed of a cereal grass from side to side. This is intended as a tribute to a hit by the Hues Corporation, since the tribe have misheard the song's title and think it is one letter shorter than it is. What do the tribe think the title of the song is?

7. By now, Des is desperate to leave the island. He attempts to build a ship but, owing to a curse on the island, anyone who attempts to build a ship finds themselves constructing what type of building instead, which, according to the official mission statement of the organisation responsible for these buildings, 'enables people to develop their full potential in mind, body and spirit'?

8. Undeterred, Des hauls the building he has just made into the sea, leaps inside it and sets sail. After months of sailing, he spies an island. He shouts to sunbathers on the beach, 'Before I disembark, I demand assurances that you are not disco-obsessed demoniacs trapped in the 1970s!' 'Don't be silly! We are modern humans!' comes the reply, but when Des disembarks he realises he has been tricked, and he is back on Disco Island. For the sunbathers all meld into one person: the Queen of Disco herself. 'How could I have been so blind!' wails Des. 'I should have realised that if you subtract one letter of the alphabet from the phrase "modern humans", you get an anagram of the Queen of Disco's name!' Which letter of the alphabet was Des referring to?

This round is out of 8.

HENRIETTA SNEEP, PHD
SPEECH THERAPIST
'FROM IMPEDIMENT
TO EMPOWERMENT'

1. Dr Sneep's first patient is Malina Griffuffensutch, who pronounces each word as if one letter of it were replaced by another letter (so 'fill' might be spoken as 'file' or 'mill' or 'fall', for instance). She reveals at one point during the session that her favourite musical is *Rick on Apes*. Which musical is she referring to?

2. Dr Sneep's next patient is Elena Herringslather, a sixty-year-old widow who can only communicate using the titles of songs from *Sgt Pepper's Lonely Hearts Club Band*. Elena is very excited to confide that she, in collaboration with her close acquaintants, has hatched a plot to have her sister evicted in four years' time. Which three song titles does she use to communicate this news? (Have half a point if you can only identify two of them.)

3. Dr Sneep's next patient is Nathania Quartermain, who always pronounces one particular letter of the alphabet as a different letter, which leads to all kinds of misunderstandings. She refers to a mixture used to coat food before deep-frying as speech used by a salesman and refers to a famous clock as a sty. Which letter does she pronounce as which other letter?

4. Dr Sneep's next patient is Eliza de Jauntenay, who, through Dr Sneep's meticulous attentions, has learnt to pronounce the words 'a' and 'the'. However, every other word she utters rhymes with the word she intends to say. As an exercise, Dr Sneep asks her to recite a quotation from her favourite film and she replies, 'Cheese shot the papaya, squeeze a merry haughty toy.' What is Eliza's favourite film?

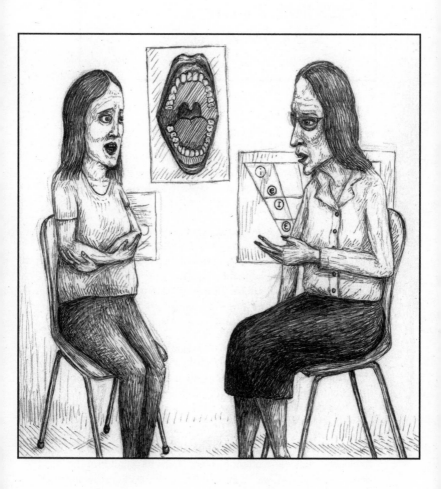

5. Dr Sneep's secretary sends in the next patient, Newland Jerrible, who pronounces every word as if it had an extra three letters added at the end (always in the same order), so that a word meaning 'part of a fish' is turned into a word meaning 'not eternal' and a word meaning 'rule' is turned into a word meaning 'set fire to again'. What are the three extra letters?

6. Every time the next patient, Catkin Snood, hears the name of Israel's third-largest city, he compulsively shouts out a word meaning 'plundering', so that the two words spoken consecutively sound like a word meaning 'pretentious'. What is the resulting word?

7. Dr Sneep wonders where her next patients, the O'Blibbleden twins, have got to and finds them alone in the corridor with their eyes closed, asking to be given someone called Lydia Beard. At first she is perplexed but then remembers that the O'Blibbleden twins replace all five-letter words with anagrams of those words, and that they are in fact in the middle of reciting something. What, specifically, are they reciting?

8. Dr Sneep's final patient of the day is young Deacon Moncur, who is incapable of pronouncing the surname of any US president and instead replaces it with the surname of a contemporaneous UK prime minister. He is clearly distracted from the therapy session as you hear him mutter, 'God Gladstone me the strength to Hamilton-Gordon my ear this evening so I can look cool, just like that film star Gascoyne-Cecil Callaghan.' Which four presidents' surnames has he attempted to pronounce in that sentence? (Have half a point for each.)

This round is out of 9.

ADVENT CALENDAR OF DOOM

A supervillain has presented you with an Advent calendar, but behind all but eight of the doors is a bomb. She has left a series of clues to the door numbers (all of which are whole numbers between 1 and 24) which conceal innocent chocolates. You may leave an answer blank, but if you get it wrong and choose a number that does not conceal a chocolate, the bomb will go off and you will score zero for the entire round.

1. This number can be seen on the cover of the Beatles album *Yellow Submarine*, is the number of a psalm which contains the line 'though I walk through the valley of the shadow of death, I will fear no evil' and was the squad number worn by David Beckham at Real Madrid as a tribute to Michael Jordan, who had worn the same number.

2. This number appears in the titles of a 1995 film, a 2004 film and a 2013 film, all of which feature Brad Pitt.

3. This number appears in the titles of a 1995 film, a 1997 film and a 2003 film, all of which feature Brad Pitt.

4. This number is the title of albums by LL Cool J, The Stranglers, Wet Wet Wet and Pearl Jam as well as being the title of a film starring Dudley Moore.

5. This is the number of syllables in a typical English-language haiku as well as the age of the Dancing Queen in the ABBA song.

6. This number can be reached by multiplying the two numbers in the title of a Dolly Parton song written for a 1980 film and then dividing the result by the number of Bob Marley's little birds.

7. This number is an anagram of a word meaning a colourless, flammable liquid.

8. This is the number of pieces each player starts with in a game of chess.

This round is out of 8.

171

CHEMICAL ELEMENT *BLIND DATE*

This round imagines an edition of the TV show Blind Date *in which a woman has to choose between eight eligible bachelors, all of whom are in fact chemical elements. Identify the elements from their responses to her questions.*

'If it was up to you to decide what we did on a date, what would you choose?'

Bachelor No. 1: 'I'd give my right "i" to hop across the Atlantic for a date with you, because I've got a feeling I can be your long-lost pal.'

Bachelor No. 2: 'My kind of dating usually ends up with someone discovering the age of an ancient specimen, but if that doesn't get you going, rest assured that I can be a girl's best friend.'

'What makes you the special one for me?'

Bachelor No. 3: 'You may associate my rod with despotic ruthlessness but one thing's for sure: if you're pumping me you're bound to get a good workout.'

Bachelor No. 4: 'If my atomic number were the jury, they'd find me guilty of being so amazing you'd want to put an "O" in front of my chemical symbol.'

'How would you treat me to make me feel loved?'

Bachelor No. 5: 'I was the first of my kind to form a compound, and that's just what I'll be doing with you tonight. I'll start with a kiss and take all your pain away.'

Bachelor No. 6: 'I'm as ungentlemanly towards women as my first three letters suggest, and as disreputable as my chemical symbol sounds – but you love it.'

'One of my favourite hobbies is going to rock concerts and getting wild. What kind of music brings out the wild child in you?'

Bachelor No. 7: 'I don't have much of an ear for music, and you may be surprised at my insistence on restraint from indulgences – but remember, without me, restraint from indulgences is nothing but lack.'

Bachelor No. 8: 'ABBA's greatest hits is my kind of album, so I really hope you dig it. I hope you dig me too – even though if you did, you'd only be in it for the money.'

This round is out of 8.

RIDDLES OF THE SPHINX

1. While strolling near Thebes one day, you encounter a fearsome Sphinx, who refuses to let you pass unless you solve her riddle. She says:

   'Solve this if you think in a clever way:
   You can eat me; likewise you can drink me.
   I may well be orange whichever way.
   What is more, I've no doubt you will think me
   A fine game you might play with a racket.
   And I have just one more fiendish clue:
   If this riddle's so hard that you can't crack it
   This word is what I'll do to you.'

   Which word is the answer to the Sphinx's riddle?

2. You solve her riddle but she will not budge. 'You told me you'd let me past if I solved your riddle!' you protest.
   'Ah,' says the Sphinx, 'but you see, there is one thing that I am known never to treat people with.'
   'What is that?'
   And the Sphinx says, *'Odd letters you'll find on a cod,*
   Even letters are a fearsome Greek god.'

   What does she mean?

3. The Sphinx then asks you this third riddle:

   'My first is in first but is not in one,
   My second is in second but is not in two,
   My third is in third but is not in three,
   My fourth is in fourth but is not in four,
   My fifth is in fifth but is not in five.
   Broadcasting brought me distinction and fame,
   So unravel this riddle and tell me my name.'

4. The Sphinx's fourth riddle is:

> *'If Wally's old magical friend is white,*
> *Then Edward Teach is black as night*
> *And a Graham Chapman film is yellow*
> *So what's an uxoricidal fellow?'*

5. No sooner have you answered this than the Sphinx asks you this fifth riddle:

> *'A large deer and a feline:*
> *You'll no doubt be wishing*
> *To turn them around*
> *So you're ready for fishing.'*

Which six-letter word is the answer to the Sphinx's riddle?

6. Infuriated by this string of riddles, you begin to shriek insults at the Sphinx. 'You're a silly, weird-looking prat!' you yell. 'What's more, that statue of you in Egypt is rubbish! It looks nothing like you!'

'Nonsense,' retorts the Sphinx, 'It's worthy of that great sculptor!'

'What great sculptor?'

> *'Remove my first letter and then you will see*
>
> *There's a day of the week that is named after me.*
>
> *Then remove my first letter and then you will hear*
>
> *A raucous great racket that batters your ear.'*

Whom is the Sphinx talking about?

7. The Sphinx then begins a seventh riddle:

> *'My first is in Little but is not in Dorrit,*
> *My second is in Barnaby but is not in Rudge—'*

but you interrupt her, saying, 'The answer may be either "lamb" or "lark".'

'How did you know that?' the Sphinx demands. 'Because I sneaked a glance at the answer sheet in your paw,' you confess.

'Very well, then, smarty pants,' says the Sphinx. 'But can you tell me which other two Dickens novels with two-word titles I was going to mention before you interrupted me?'

8. Having solved the Sphinx's seventh riddle, you demand, 'What can I do to stop you bombarding me with these cursed riddles?'

'There is a type of object I cherish above all other things. Bring me one such object and no more riddles you will hear from me.'

'What is the object?' you demand, and she replies:

> *'The first letter of what you must bring to me now*
> *Is the speed of light in a void,*
> *Then follows a word for a curse or a vow*
> *Then a feeling you get when annoyed.'*

You happen to be carrying one such object in your bag and present it to the Sphinx. She squeals with delight and immediately allows you to pass. Her exuberant giggles ring in your ears as you continue on your way.

This round is out of 8.

GROUNDHOG DAY

1. Phil, a jaded weatherman, awakes on February 2nd once again to the radio playing 'I Got You Babe'. How does Gangkhar Puensum in Bhutan contradict a line Phil hears in the song, unless the line's triple negative is interpreted literally?

2. A man bounds up to Phil and introduces himself as Ned Ryerson, an old classmate who sells insurance. He bears a marked resemblance to the teacher Sandy Ryerson, a character in which US TV series? If the letter 'k' is added to the end of the series' name, it denotes a fan of the series.

3. 'I've got a doozy of a question for you!' enthuses Ned. 'What's the smallest positive number divisible by 1, 2, 3, 4, 5 and 6? Think you can guess, Phil?'

4. Bidding a hasty goodbye to Ned, Phil is intrigued by his sweet-natured producer Rita, and when he asks what she most wants from the future, she replies that she wants to hear the pitter-patter of tiny feet. Phil misconstrues her words as a wish to visit which island, which has its capital at Mildendo and whose most famous visitor was named Lemuel?

5. As she walks away, exasperated, Phil realises what she really wanted: a four-letter word which is also the title of a Justin Bieber song overtaken by 'Gangnam Style' in 2012 to become the most watched YouTube video. What word is Phil thinking of?

6. Phil retreats to a cafe, where he meets an attractive woman named Nancy and asks what quality she most admires in a man. She responds cryptically: 'Take the opposite of a Hitchcock film, for short, followed by the biggest Ben and finally frozen, then turn it all around.' What quality is she alluding to?

7. He returns to his hotel, where he joins other guests watching a TV quiz. 'If my friend were the Pope and he were called Pope Pop, how could I describe his name?' asks the host. Phil responds with which ten-letter answer, which can also refer to the date of Groundhog Day in 2020?

8. 'Two shirts...' begins the quiz show host, but Phil interrupts. 'I've heard this question a hundred times. Here's a better two shirts question: who was said to have worn two shirts outside the Banqueting House in Whitehall to avoid shivering with cold that might have been mistaken for fear?'

1. Phil, a jaded weatherman, awakes on February 2nd once again to the radio playing 'I Got You Babe'. He recalls the 1993 version of the song by Cher and which animated duo, both of whom are voiced by their creator Mike Judge?

2. Increasingly unhinged by his ever-repeating existence, Phil believes himself to be both Elvis's continually crying canine and a character who never ages as he grows morally corrupt. 'Today's beginnings are shifting...' he mutters as he confers what three-word nickname upon himself?

3. He cajoles some men he meets in a bowling alley into accompanying him on a terrifying joyride. 'It's fate that I crash this car!' he shrieks. 'The first syllable of the shape of the car sounds like a word meaning "destroy" and the rest of the word means "state of confusion"!' Which word is Phil thinking of, which describes the shape of the car?

4. Staggering from the scene of the crash, he returns to his hotel, where he joins other guests watching a TV quiz. 'If my friend were the Pope and he were called Pope Pop, how could I describe his name?' asks the host. This time Phil responds with an equally valid answer which is spelt identically to the last answer he gave to this question, except that it is missing one letter and has spaces added. What is Phil's answer?

5. 'Two shirts used in which film were sold at auction for over $100,000?' continues the host. 'Is it *Sense and Sensibility*, *Hulk* or *Brokeback Mountain*?'

6. Phil takes up piano lessons. At first he misses the keys every time, instead hitting nearby objects which produce an array of noises: *ROOAR! BLUBBUB! FLOOF! SPAP! TWEET! PIPE! WAWL! PLEEP!* 'Just think of Pope Pop,' says the teacher, 'and make the music reflect that. Take comfort from the obstacles you find in your path.' What reassuring message does Phil take from this?

7. Phil meets up with Nancy, impressing her with his resolute manner. He invites her to the cinema, and confesses that his favourite film characters are Harris K. Telemacher in *L.A. Story*, Brick Tamland in *Anchorman* and Suzanne Stone in *To Die For*. What do they have in common?

8. Though Nancy is responsive to Phil's charms, he feels strangely empty, makes his excuses and seeks out Rita. 'I've always dreamed of visiting the capital of an island nation,' she sighs. 'One you can put "Wood" after...' 'To make a British comedian's name?' interrupts Phil. 'I know just the one you're thinking of.' And he tells her. But this was not what Rita had been thinking of, and she leaves with a shudder. Which city had Phil named?

1. Phil, a jaded weatherman, awakes on February 2nd once again to the radio playing 'I Got You Babe'. It reminds him of a song used in the series *Russian Doll* every time the main character's time loop restarts by which American singer-songwriter, in whose London flat Cass Elliot and Keith Moon both died?

2. Witnessing the ceremony in which the groundhog predicts six more weeks of winter, Phil gives a rousingly informative speech about how which alternative name for the groundhog is derived from a word in an Algonquian language and as such is unrelated to a fibrous substance or throwing?

3. He rushes to his piano lesson, where his teacher has some sage advice. 'If you find a swampy bog, go back to start again. If you find a source of pain, go back to make music from which country?' What does Phil accurately answer?

4. He returns to his hotel, where he joins other guests watching a TV quiz. 'Two shirts used in which film were sold at auction for over $100,000?' asks the host. 'Is it *Sense and Sensibility*, *Hulk* or *Brokeback Mountain*?' The contestant says the right answer. 'Good, she got the core film,' comments Phil, only then realizing that he is still traumatised from his earlier car crash and was unable to say a string of letters. Which four words was Phil trying to say instead of 'core film'?

5. Phil impresses Rita with his virtuosic piano-playing at a party, and then the two of them dance. 'I've found meaning at last!' he exclaims. He orders from the bar: 'Get me a Spanish hard yellow fruit, a French collar and a German helper of Santa

Claus! How much does that come to?' What number does the bartender say?

6. Phil is congratulated by a couple for having performed what earlier that day? A man credited for the discovery of this successfully performed it at the age of 96 on a fellow resident of his retirement home.

7. As Phil and Rita are about to kiss, Phil's old classmate Ned interrupts. 'I never got to tell you all about my insurance! Take both of your answers so far which have been numbers and add them up, then convert that into Roman numerals! Add your answers to the two questions found immediately after you said goodbye to me and you'll get an anagram of my favourite kind of insurance!' What is Ned's favourite kind of insurance?

8. Rita and Phil adjourn to his hotel room. 'I've always dreamed of visiting the capital of an island nation,' she sighs. 'One you can put 'Wood' after...' 'To make a part of London?' interrupts Phil. 'I know just the one you're thinking of.' And he tells her. 'That's quite right!' says Rita, and they declare their love for one another. Which city had Phil named?

When Phil awakes the following morning, Rita is beside him. He has found true happiness and broken free of the time loop.

This round is out of 24.

THE MURDER MYSTERY

Aristotle Maria Macks

Dolores Sesquave

Lady Arabella
Truckleshaw

Dr K. N. Frederalfred

Trixie LaVetch

Claudiella Truckleshaw

Dino Canard

Hugo Actovius

Lyxa Actovius

Sir Harbledon
Truckleshaw (deceased)

TO SET THE SCENE:

Rumours abound that **Lady Arabella Truckleshaw** lives simply to torment **Sir Harbledon**. On this occasion she has invited their older daughter **Claudiella**, a purveyor of exquisite jellies, to dinner along with her girlfriend **Trixie**, a motorcycle stunt performer, and **Dolores**, Claudiella's childhood governess turned personal assistant, whose nervous disposition is exacerbated by Claudiella's erratic mood swings. Trixie tosses away the smoked mackerel proffered by **Mr Macks**, the butler, and orders a hamburger, which is brought by deliveryman **Dino**. Dino stays for the remainder of the evening, responding to any hints that he should leave by flipping a coin and murmuring cryptic proverbs. Sir Harbledon begins to twitch from the stress, at which point Lady Arabella declares a medical emergency and summons **Dr Frederalfred**, a man Sir Harbledon detests owing to his tendency to criticise Sir Harbeldon's mackerel. In the midst of the cheese course, younger daughter **Lyxa** bursts in with **Hugo Actovius**. No one had heard a trace of them for ten years. Actovius was once the family cook, but one day he prepared a plate of devilled eggs so exquisite that he was driven mad, and was kept on at the house as an act of charity – until he eloped with Lyxa. As Lyxa savours the brie that Hugo has inserted into his ears, Sir Harbledon bellows that dinner is over and storms out. The rest of the party disperse and roam through the manor, marvelling at its sinister architectural quirks – until Sir Harbledon's lifeless body is discovered. With his dying breath, Sir Harbledon has scrawled in his own blood a series of quiz questions providing clues to the circumstances of his murder. *This is that quiz.*

The floor plan below shows where Sir Harbledon's body was discovered. It is clear, however, that the body has been moved. Use the answers to **Round 1** to retrace the murderer's footsteps, starting from the square where the body now lies. Each answer begins with 'N', 'E', 'S' or 'W', indicating whether you should go north, east, south or west. The number of squares you need to move each time corresponds to the number of letters in the answer (including the first letter). Each dotted line on the floor plan respresents a door, which is the only entrance or exit to the room it points to. Always walk past doors unless the direction you are sent in by an answer leads you through a door. The room you should find yourself in at the end of Round 1 is where the murder took place.

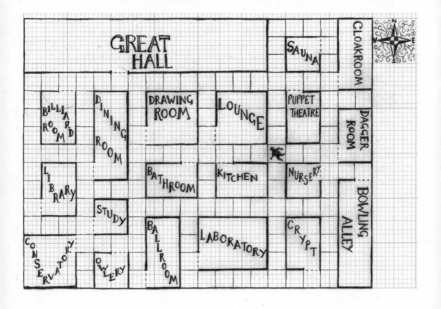

THE MURDER MYSTERY, ROUND 1

1. The name of which country becomes the name of a neighbouring country if the last two letters are removed?

2. Every spring, which East Anglian city has a festival to celebrate the fish after which the city is thought to be named?

3. The name of which city appears in the punning title of a Bryan Talbot graphic novel exploring the links between the world of Lewis Carroll and the north-east of England?

4. William Astor, who initiated the building of a New York hotel where a famous salad was invented in 1893, had what middle name?

5. 'I wanted a name that was kind of beautiful or nice and pretty instead of a mean, raunchy punk-rock name', said the lead singer of which grunge band?

6. Which is the only US state named after a US president?

7. Which product, named after a horse, was known by a different name in the UK and Ireland until 1990, supposedly because the original American name sounded too much like a British word for an undergarment?

8. Which 1815 novel was criticised by Maria Edgeworth, a contemporary of its author, as having a flimsy plot, consisting simply of the title character realising that a man she intended for her friend in fact has designs on her and the man is then affronted?

This round is out of 8.

THE MURDER MYSTERY, ROUND 2

*In **Round 2**, the answers come in pairs. The second answer in each pair is an anagram of the first, but with one extra letter. The extra letters spell out the motive for the murder.*

1a. The world's first Tuareg-language fiction film, the title of which translates literally as 'Rain the colour of blue with a little red in it', is a homage to a 1984 film which featured which musician starring as 'The Kid'? (I want the one-word name by which this musician is most commonly known.)

1b. What was the surname of the notorious doctor hanged in 1910 for the murder of his wife Cora?

2a. What is the nickname of a character in the series *Fresh Meat* as well as the name of a US state bordering Idaho and California?

2b. Which herb, which is closely related to marjoram, is commonly used in Italian and Greek cuisine to flavour tomato dishes and grilled meats?

3a. The name of which building in Rome, completed during the reign of the Emperor Hadrian, can also be used to mean a group of famous or distinguished people?

3b. According to Melina Mercouri, who served as Greek Minister for Culture, the very name of Greece is immediately associated with what? It was described by Picasso as 'really only a farmyard over which someone put a roof'.

4a. Which surname is shared by the author of *Goodbye, Mr Chips* and *Lost Horizon* and a star of the TV series *The Simple Life*?

4b. Which seven letters may follow East, Mid or West to form the names of three shires of Scotland?

5a. Which nine-letter word can refer to one of the three major stages of the oil and gas industry as well as being a situation in which, according to a proverb, it is inadvisable to change horses?

5b. Which word may refer to an enemy of the X-Men, a game involving pegs or a TV quiz show?

6a. Which word for a dock or harbour can also be used as a first name? People with this name include a Serbian performance artist and the author of *A Short History of Tractors in Ukrainian*.

6b. Which country, if you put the letters 'py' in front of its name, becomes a dangerous compulsion?

7a. The critic Walter Kerr famously dismissed a theatrical adaptation of Christopher Isherwood's *Goodbye to Berlin* with the three-word review 'Me no Leica', which was a pun on the play's title being *I am a* what?

7b. The name of which band, which had a hit with 'A Horse with No Name', is also the first name of the actress who played Ugly Betty?

8a. Which English cathedral city is also the first name of the twenty-first US president?

8b. What is the shared title of a song on Leonard Cohen's first album and a Channel 4 series starring Andrew Lincoln, which aired between 2001 and 2004?

This round is out of 16.

THE MURDER MYSTERY, ROUND 3

The answers to this round will help you identify which one of the weapons clued on the next two pages killed Sir Harbledon.

1. The fictional character John Clayton, Viscount Greystoke, is better known by what name, which translates as 'white skin'?

2. Which midfielder, whose clubs have included Southampton and Liverpool, scored the only goal of Sam Allardyce's tenure as England manager?

3. Which country, according to Marshall McLuhan, one of its most famous intellectuals, is 'the only country in the world that knows how to live without an identity'?

4. The play *Everybody Comes to Rick's* was adapted into which 1940s film?

5. In 2008, the mayor of which Turkish city announced plans to sue film director Christopher Nolan over the unauthorised use of his city's name?

6. Which word may refer to a vehicle, a group of people travelling together, a jazz standard associated with Duke Ellington or a progressive rock band from Kent?

7. When Edward Albee's *Who's Afraid of Virginia Woolf?* was first performed in Prague, Virginia Woolf was replaced by which author in the play's title?

8. Which Tim Burton film was inspired by a set of extremely violent trading cards released in 1962?

This round is out of 8.

REBUS: WEAPONS

The following visual clues, read aloud, will form the names of the eight weapons discovered at the manor. (For instance, a picture of a bay followed by a picture of Annette Bening would form 'bayonet'.) Though some of these weapons are not usually fatal, you know that one of them is the murder weapon. **Identify the eight weapons.** *You should be able to ascertain which one of them is the murder weapon from* **Round 3**, *as it is the only one that could be a valid answer in that round (in which all of the answers have a hidden connection).*

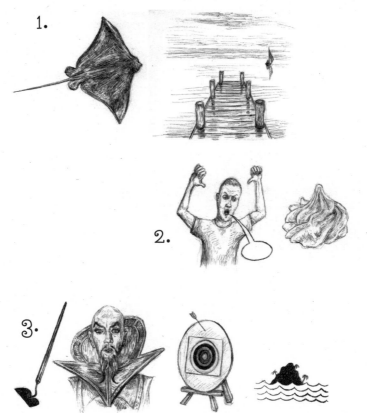

1.

2.

3.

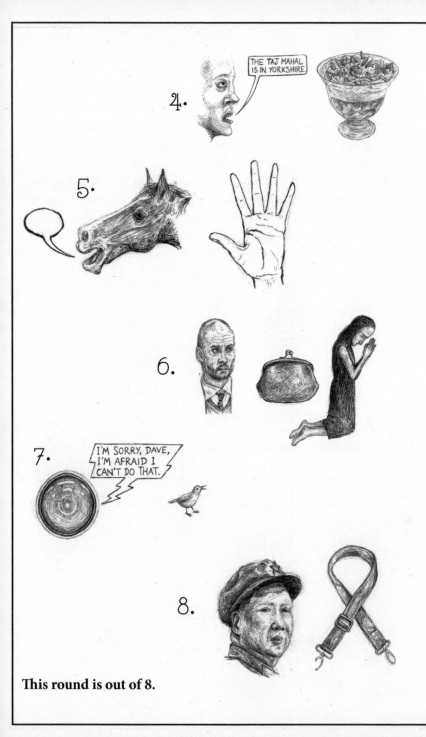

4.

5.

6.

7.

8.

This round is out of 8.

*In **Round 4**, each question provides a clue to a letter and number. Whenever you answer a question, draw a dot in the centre of the grid reference corresponding to the answer. By joining up the dots in order of when the questions were asked, you will form a picture of the killer's face.*

	A	B	C	D	E	F	G	H	I	J	K	L
1												
2												
3												
4												
5												
6												
7												
8												
9												
10												
11												
12												

THE MURDER MYSTERY, ROUND 4

1. The first grid reference can be found in the name of a vehicle launched by Clive Sinclair in 1985 and by Citroën in 2001.

2. Three letters can be placed in front of the words 'sting' and 'gent' or inserted into the words 'sly' and 'cost' to make four new words. The grid reference can be found if you treat the last two of these letters as a Roman numeral.

3. The next grid reference is a name given to the schooling system practised in the United States, which is formed from the first letter of a class typically attended by 5–6 year olds followed by a number corresponding to the last grade attended by high school students.

4. If you remove the letter 'a' from the first name shared by the killer of Barry Evans in *EastEnders*, the secretary to the original Ghostbusters, and a character played by Elle Macpherson in *Friends*, you will get the next grid reference.

5. The next grid reference begins with a letter that cannot be found on the periodic table and the grid reference as a whole rhymes with something Billy Bragg, Christina Aguilera and John Major wished to return to.

6. A Christmas film from 2003 starring Will Ferrell and the surname of the British designer known for his work with Apple combine to sound like the name of the next grid reference.

7. The next grid reference is formed from the single initial by which the narrator of a humorous 1889 novel is referred to, followed by the number of characters in the novel (human or otherwise) who take a trip up the Thames.

8. For the next grid reference, remove the last two letters from the name of a character who has appeared in more than ten feature films and is voiced by British actor Anthony Daniels.

9. The next grid reference, if spoken in a style associated with the Reverend Spooner, would sound like an invitation to dance extended to a woman who has presented Radio 4's *Saturday Live* and *The Listening Project* and co-hosted *Fortunately…* with Jane Garvey.

10. The next grid reference is spelt out by the word missing from these two quotations. Firstly, from Dylan Thomas's 'Do Not Go Gentle Into That Good Night', 'And you, my father, there on the sad _____' and secondly, a baffling quotation from *Match of the Day*'s Mark Lawrenson, 'Michael Owen isn't the tallest of lads, but his _____ more than makes up for that'.

11. The next grid reference is formed from a letter found in the name of only one US state, followed by the number of US states that contain the letter 'p'.*

12. The next grid reference is made up of the only letter not found in the sentence 'Albert, Duke of Saxony owes opaque jam to Hugo Chávez' and the number of points this letter is worth in *Scrabble*.

13. Subtract six, in Roman numerals, from a word meaning 'relating to cattle' to spell out the next grid reference.

14. The next grid reference will lead you to King's Lynn from London Bridge, via Cambridge.

15. The next grid reference is a group which released the singles 'Purple Pills' and 'My Band' and which featured Eminem as a member.

16. Take the third country in Africa in alphabetical order and move its second letter to the end in order to reveal the final grid reference.

This round is out of 16.

---

*   Not including Rhode Island, which dropped 'Providence Plantations' from its official name in 2020. Puerto Rico, which at the time of writing has not been declared a US state despite overwhelmingly voting to become one in a 2017 referendum, doesn't count either.

And Finally...

For two points each, identify:

1. The room in which the murder took place
2. The motive for the murder
3. The murder weapon
4. The murderer

This round is out of 8.

195

TIE BREAKERS

It helps to have one of these questions up your sleeve if you're compiling a quiz. The player or team whose guess is closest to the correct answer wins.

1. A project determines the size of rappers' vocabulary by calculating the number of words which occur only once among the first 35,000 words of their lyrics. The project concluded that Aesop Rock had by far the widest vocabulary, with how many unique words out of 35,000?

2. How many people speak Cornish as their main language, according to the 2011 Census?

3. Which year saw the first recorded usage of OMG as an abbreviation for 'Oh my God'?

4. In the 2001 single 'Can't Get You Out Of My Head', how many times in total does Kylie Minogue sing the word 'la'?

5. In the 1961 Disney animation *One Hundred and One Dalmatians*, how many spots do the Dalmatians have between them?

6. In 1989 a man bet £30 that by the year 2000 Cliff Richard would have been knighted, the band U2 would still be together and that *EastEnders*, *Neighbours* and *Home and Away* would still be on television. How much money did he win (not adjusted for inflation)?

7. According to John R. Greenfield's *Dictionary of British Literary Characters*, how many named characters did Charles Dickens create?

8. In the classic version of the board game *Cluedo*, how many possible solutions are there?

ANSWERS

PART ONE: ALL FUN AND GAMES

...UNTIL SOMEONE LOSES AN 'I'

1. Berber and beriberi

2. Savour and saviour

3. Fester and feistier

4. Dares (as in 'Who Dares Wins') and dairies

5. Refer and reifier

6. Harness and hairiness

7. Wrest and wiriest

8. Nantes and inanities

REBUS: GAMES

1. Winking murder (wing; king; murder [of crows])

2. Articulate ('Arr!'; tick; Yule; eight)

3. Cricket ([Francis] Crick; [Cousin] Itt [from the Addams Family])

4. Backgammon (back; gammon)

5. Hide and seek ([Joseph] Haydn; Sikh)

6. Baseball (bay; [Timothy] Spall)

7. Archery (Art [Garfunkel]; Cherie [Blair])

8. I spy (ice pie)

HUNT THE SYNONYMS

1. Distress and suffering

2. Pair and duo*

3. Enrage and madden

4. Sacred and holy

5. Chasm and gulf

6. Award and prize

7. Certain and sure

8. Dedicate and devote

IF THIS IS THE ANSWER, WHAT'S THE QUESTION?

1. *Who's Afraid of Virginia Woolf?*

2. *Who Framed Roger Rabbit***

3. Is the Pope a Catholic?

4. Which came first: the chicken or the egg?

5. Why is a raven like a writing desk? (From *Alice's Adventures in Wonderland*)***

6. 'Should I Stay or Should I Go' (by the Clash)

7. *Dude, Where's my Car?*

8. How much wood would a woodchuck chuck if a woodchuck could chuck wood?

---

*   When I posed this question to the pub, one team came up with 'pail and jug', which I hadn't considered at the time but reluctantly accepted, though I've now come to the opinion that they're not synonymous enough to count.

**   The reason for the film's title lacking a question mark is supposedly down to a Hollywood superstition that question marks in film titles bring bad luck.

*** In a preface to the 1896 edition, Lewis Carroll proposed the solution, 'Because it can produce a few notes, tho they are very flat; and it is nevar put with the wrong end in front.' Later editions corrected 'nevar' ('raven' backwards) to 'never', rendering this solution rather confusing.

DOCTOR, DOCTOR

1. Doctor Foster (from the nursery rhyme beginning, 'Doctor Foster went to Gloucester...')

2. Dr Jones (from the song by Aqua)

3. Dr No*

4. Doctor Robert (from the Beatles song)

5. Dr Eggman, alias Dr Robotnik (in the *Sonic the Hedgehog* franchise)**

6. Dr Jekyll

7. Dr Seuss

8. Dr Strangelove

WHAT'S THE DIFFERENCE? (NO. 1)

1. One's Bruce Lee and the other's loose Brie

2. One's a pack of lies and the other's a lack of pies

3. One's a curious foreigner and the other's a furious coroner

4. One's a jack of all trades and the other's a track of all jades***

5. One's *Master of Puppets* and the other's a pastor of Muppets

6. One's a pearl earring and the other's an earl peering

7. One's *The First Wives Club* and the other's the worst fives club

8. One's *Gulliver's Travels* and the other's Tulliver's gravels (Maggie Tulliver being the heroine of *The Mill on the Floss*)

....

*   Dr No has pincers in the novel, which were upgraded to metal hands in the film. The film also gives him a (slightly) more dignified death, as the novel sees him buried alive in guano. When I posed this question to the pub, Spider-Man villain Dr Octopus proved a popular answer – though he has metal pincers *as well as* hands, not instead of them.

**   Sonic's archenemy was always known as Dr Robotnik in English until 1999, when *Sonic Adventure* permanently changed his name. He has always been known as Dr Eggman in Japan.

***   When I posed this question to the pub, one team came up with 'One's Thomas More and the other's Momma's tour', which I rather enjoyed.

ROUND THE WORLD TRICK OR TREAT

1. Japan

2. Trick

3. Ireland

4. Trick

5. Trick

6. Germany*

7. Philippines

8. Trick

PROS AND CONS

1. Province and convince

2. Protest and contest

3. Progress and congress

4. Profound and confound

5. Profuse and confuse

6. Product and conduct

7. Procession and concession

8. Proscription and conscription

....
*   The lines are from Goethe's *Faust* (translated by Philip Wayne).

SUM FUN WITH ROMAN NUMERALS

1. Cyst + CLI = cyclist

2. Deer + LIV = deliver

3. Convey + XL = convexly

4. Cot + MMI = commit

5. Boer + X = boxer

6. Lash + VI = lavish

7. Quote + IX = Quixote

8. Coerce + MM = commerce

MONOPOLY

Old Kent Road: Rochester

Whitechapel Road: Jackson Pollock

Water Works: Stopcocks (or, more fully, Stopcocks Women Plumbers)

Electric Company: The Taser (an acronym for 'Thomas A. Swift's Electric Rifle')[*]

Fleet Street: The Sweeney (from 'Sweeney Todd')

Strand: British actors who had been nominated for the Oscars that year (Charlotte Rampling, Tom Hardy, Eddie Redmayne, Christian Bale, Mark Rylance and Kate Winslet)

Park Lane: Mohamed Al-Fayed (the deaths were of Al-Fayed's son Dodi and Princess Diana, with the 'Fred West-style psychopath' and 'gangster in a tiara' being a reference to Prince Philip and Elizabeth II)

Mayfair: *Hangover Square*

....
[*]   Cover conferred a middle initial on Tom Swift for the sole purpose of making the acronym easier to pronounce.

WHAT'S THE DIFFERENCE? (NO. 2)

1. One's writer's block and the other's blighter's rock

2. One's 'What's life?' and the other's Lot's wife

3. One's Buster Keaton and the other's Custer beaten

4. One's letterbox and the other's better locks

5. One's Morse code and the other's coarse mode

6. One's the Gold Coast and the other's a cold ghost

7. One's feeling the heat and the other's healing the feet

8. One's 'How Much Is That Doggy in the Window' and the other's 'How Dutch Is That Moggy in the Window?'

PART TWO: GENERAL FIENDISHNESS

A SOFT PILCHARD TOWEL

1. Solo (Napoleon and Han) – Norway (Oslo)

2. Mali – Peru (Lima)

3. (Carl) Barât (the line-up of the Libertines) – Morocco (Rabat)

4. Tobago (thought to be derived from 'tobacco') – Colombia (Bogotá)

5. Animal (from the Muppets) – Philippines (Manila)

6. Louse – South Korea (Seoul)

7. Anther – Iran (Tehran)

8. Saunas – Bahamas (Nassau)

REBUS: MUSIC MAKERS

1. Bo Diddley (bowed idli)

2. Ringo Starr (ring; ghost; tar)

3. Coolio ('Coo!'; [zodiacal symbol for] Leo)

4. Eminem ([Tracey] Emin; M [as portrayed by Judi Dench])

5. LL Cool J* (Elle [Macpherson]; elk; 'ooljay' [Pig Latin for 'jewel'])

6. Bombay Bicycle Club (bomb; Babe [from the 1995 film of the same name]; icicle; club)

7. Counting Crows (Count [von Count, from *Sesame Street*]; ink; rose])

8. Camper Van Beethoven (Cam; perv; [Princess] Anne; bait; hoe; [John] Venn)

....

* James Todd Smith's stage name is an abbreviation of 'Ladies Love Cool James'.

PREMATURE OBITUARIES

1. Terry Gilliam[*]

2. Ronald Reagan

3. Queen Elizabeth the Queen Mother's

4. Alfred Nobel's[**]

5. James Earl Jones (James Earl Ray was convicted of the assassination)[***]

6. Marcus Garvey

7. Alice Cooper

8. Ernest Hemingway

GENERAL FIENDISHNESS (NO. 1)

1. Abraham Lincoln (It is a line from the play *Our American Cousin* by Tom Taylor, which Lincoln was watching.)

2. Hotshots

3. A bee's knee[****]

4. The letters are written in alphabetical order

....

[*]   Gilliam renounced his US citizenship in 2006, partly in protest at George W. Bush and partly to save money on taxes.

[**]   The story of Nobel reading his own obituary and having a crisis of conscience has been widely circulated and was recounted by Al Gore in his Nobel Lecture. However, although Olov Amelin, the director of Stockholm's Nobel Museum, has confirmed that the French press did indeed run erroneous obituaries of Nobel after his brother's death, there is no evidence to suggest that this inspired the establishment of the Nobel Prizes. The most common version of the story centres on an obituary in the newspaper *Ideotie Quotidienne*, which was headlined, 'The merchant of death is dead' and began, 'Dr Alfred Nobel, who made his fortune by finding ways to kill more people faster than ever before, died yesterday.' A 2013 article in *Smithsonian* magazine found that every telling of the story relied on these same two quotations, and that *Ideotie Quotidienne* 'basically doesn't exist except attached to this tale'.

[***] An even more unfortunate confusion occurred in 2002, when a plaque intended to honour Jones as part an event marking Martin Luther King Day in Lauderhill, Florida, was engraved with the words, 'Thank you James Earl Ray for keeping the dream alive'.

[****] At the time of writing, ASML, a Dutch corporation which produces lithography machines used to make microchips, is the holder of the 'world's smallest advertisement' record, with an advert on a silicon wafer reading, 'To Truly Go Small You Have To Think Big #Smallest_AD ASML'.

5. Vincent van Gogh's ear*

6. Launch a single ship (It is a reference to Christopher Marlowe's *Doctor Faustus*, in which Faustus addresses Helen of Troy with the words, 'Was this the face that launch'd a thousand ships/ and burnt the topless towers of Ilium?')

7. 'Mambo No. 5' (a Lou Bega reworking of a Dámaso Pérez Prado song, with the chorus beginning 'A little bit of Monica in my life')

8. Usher and Christoph Waltz

FOOT IN MOUTH

1. Glenn Hoddle**

2. Alicia Silverstone (*Clueless* being the film in question)

3. Jamie Redknapp***

4. Mitt Romney

5. Naomi Campbell

6. Tracey Emin

7. Barack Obama

8. Teletubbies

----

*   In 2016 the recipient of the ear was finally identified as Gabrielle Berlatier, a farmer's daughter who was working as a maid in a brothel. In the same year a letter from van Gogh's doctor was discovered confirming that he had severed the whole ear and not (as had previously been speculated) just the lobe.
**   He was fired as England manager after suggesting that the disabled were paying for their sins in previous lives.
***   Not only did he overuse the word 'literally' but he failed to use the word 'literally' when a sentence could really have benefited from it, as in 'Peter Schmeichel will be like a father figure to Kasper Schmeichel.'

THE ONE AND ONLY

1. Mozambique

2. Saint Lucia

3. A dwarf and a giant*

4. Bart Simpson

5. Westward Ho!**

6. Liza Minnelli (her parents were Vincente Minnelli and Judy Garland)***

7. *Wisden Cricketers' Almanack*

8. Her head was displayed on a spike at London Bridge

GENERAL FIENDISHNESS (NO. 2)

1. Irving (Irving Berlin/Washington Irving)

2. Mullet (the song being 'Mullet Head')

3. *SpongeBob SquarePants*

4. Jones (*Tom Jones* by Henry Fielding and *Bridget Jones's Diary* by Helen Fielding)

5. The Land of Nod

6. 1009 (MIX)

7. Debagged

8. They can walk – or in the petrel's case, appear to walk – on water

....

*   He was just under 4'10" on his 21st birthday but grew to over 7 feet tall over the next decade. He was 7'8" at the time of his death.

**   Quebec's St-Louis-du-Ha! Ha! has the honour of being the only town in the world with two exclamation marks in its name.

***   Vincente Minnelli received the Best Director Oscar for *Gigi*; Judy Garland won a Juvenile Oscar (officially the Academy Juvenile Award, which was sporadically awarded between 1934 and 1960) for her work in *The Wizard of Oz* and *Babes in Arms*, and was portrayed by Renée Zellweger in *Judy*. Liza Minnelli (whose first husband, Peter Allen, went on to win an Oscar for co-writing the main theme to *Arthur*) won Best Actress for *Cabaret*.

THE OSCARS

1. Ray Charles; Jamie Foxx (in *Ray*)

2. Truman Capote; Philip Seymour Hoffman (in *Capote*). The book adapted by Blake Edwards was *Breakfast at Tiffany's*

3. Idi Amin*; Forest Whitaker (in *The Last King of Scotland*)

4. Virginia Woolf; Nicole Kidman (in *The Hours*)

5. Henry VIII; Charles Laughton (in *The Private Life of Henry VIII*)

6. Hamlet; Laurence Olivier (in *Hamlet*)

7. Eleanor of Aquitaine (also called Eleanor of Guyenne); Katharine Hepburn (in *The Lion in Winter*)

8. Margaret Thatcher; Meryl Streep (in *The Iron Lady*)

LOST IN TRANSLATION

1. *Girl, Interrupted*

2. *Cloudy with a Chance of Meatballs*

3. *Bringing up Baby*

4. *The Producers*

5. *Weekend at Bernie's*

6. *Eternal Sunshine of the Spotless Mind*

7. *Some Like It Hot*

8. *Don't Look Now*

---

*   Idi Amin's full title was His Excellency, President for Life, Field Marshal Al Hadji Doctor Idi Amin Dada, VC, DSO, MC, Lord of All the Beasts of the Earth and Fishes of the Seas, and Conqueror of the British Empire in Africa in General and Uganda in Particular. A friend of mine pointed out that 'damn' and 'Idi Amin' would have been a good pair of answers for the very first round of this book.

REBUS: THE BEATLES

1. 'Day Tripper' (date; [Jack the] Ripper)

2. 'Because' ([logo for] Bic; Oz)

3. 'Eleanor Rigby' (*Elle* [magazine]; inner; rig; bee)

4. 'Honey Pie' ([Attila the] Hun [as depicted in *Night at the Museum*]; 'Neep? Aye!')

5. 'I'm Only Sleeping' (eye; moan; lease; leaping)

6. 'I Saw Her Standing There' (ice; [expression of] awe; hearse; tan; ding; 'There'*)

7. 'Magical Mystery Tour' (Madge**; ickle; miss; treat; ore)

GENERAL FIENDISHNESS (NO. 3)

1. Angora (an old name for Ankara)

2. Napoleon Dynamite***

3. A jockstrap

4. Going over Niagara Falls in a barrel

5. Called him Al ('You Can Call Me Al')****

6. The board game *Operation*

7. A paperclip

8. Castor*****

---

* The drawing illustrating 'There' is based on a detail from a Walter Langley painting.

** Madonna disliked the nickname Madge, claiming in an interview that she left England partly to escape it. It was used by the British press as well as her ex-husband Guy Ritchie, who reportedly told her it was short for 'Your Majesty'.

*** Hess, a Mormon, claims that he took the name from a man he met while doing missionary work.

**** Simon also named his song 'Mother and Child Reunion' after a chicken-and-egg dish on a Chinese restaurant's menu.

***** Castor, Olive and Olive's boyfriend Ham Gravy (also known as Harold Hamgravy) were the central figures of E. C. Segar's comic strip *Thimble Theatre* before the debut of Popeye, who was originally intended to be a minor character.

NAMESAKES

1. Brian Cox

2. Taylor Swift*

3. Elizabeth Taylor

4. David Mitchell

5. Steve McQueen

6. Montana (Helena is capital of Montana; Cyrus the Great founded the Achaemenid Empire and Miley Cyrus played Hannah Montana)

7. Don Draper (from *Mad Men*, born Richard Whitman**)

8. Katie Perry***

THE *MAIL* AND THE *MASTERPIECES*

1. *Dracula*, Bram Stoker

2. *The Wind in the Willows*, Kenneth Grahame

3. *Wuthering Heights*, Emily Brontë

4. *The Hound of the Baskervilles*, Arthur Conan Doyle

5. *Gulliver's Travels*, Jonathan Swift

6. *The BFG*, Roald Dahl

7. *Jude the Obscure*, Thomas Hardy

8. *Pride and Prejudice*, Jane Austen

....

*   Singer-songwriter Taylor Swift gained a great deal of publicity from the 2009 MTV Video Music Awards owing to the infamous moment when, in the middle of her acceptance speech for the Best Female Video award, Kanye West seized the microphone and announced that the award should have gone to Beyoncé instead.

**   The hotel chain's offer was not extended to people called Richard Whitman.

***   Katy Perry was originally Katy Hudson, but adopted Perry as her stage surname (from her mother's maiden name) to avoid confusion with Kate Hudson. Perry hails from a devoutly religious family, to the extent that her parents insisted on calling devilled eggs 'angelled eggs' and avoided using the word 'lucky' because it was too reminiscent of 'Lucifer'. Her first album was the Christian rock record *Katy Hudson*.

COOKING WITH THE STARS

1. Maya Angelou

2. Sheryl Crow*

3. Salvador Dalí

4. Coolio**

5. Yul Brynner***

6. Alicia Silverstone (the film role was Batgirl in *Batman and Robin*)

7. Liberace

8. Sarah Ferguson, the Duchess of York

REBUS: PROFESSIONS

1. Physiotherapist (fizzy oath; era [pronounced American-style, with a short 'e']; pissed)

2. Puppeteer (pup; pit; tear)

3. Window cleaner (wind; oak; leaner)

4. Carpenter (car; [Harold] Pinter)

5. Historian (hiss; store; Ian [McKellen])

6. Optician (op; [copy of self-portrait by] Titian)

7. Flight engineer (fly; ten; gin; ear)

GENERAL FIENDISHNESS (NO. 4)

1. The G-spot

2. Shaggy

3. Amatory (becoming 'defamatory')

....

*   The title is a play on Crow's song 'If It Makes You Happy'.

**   According to the endlessly quotable *Cookin' with Coolio*, '[E]verything I cook tastes better than yo momma's nipples'.

***   The subtitle is a play on the Brynner film *The King and I*.

4. *Inspector Morse* ('Morse' is spelt out in Morse code)[*]

5. *The Graduate*

6. Ecclesiastes

7. Hannah Montana[**]

8. Branwell Brontë

IT TAKES TWO

1. Jodie Foster and Natalie Portman (a reference to *Taxi Driver* and *Léon: The Professional*, and to their directorial debuts *Little Man Tate* and *A Tale of Love and Darkness*)

2. The Proclaimers (Charlie and Craig Reid) and the Jesus and Mary Chain (Jim and William Reid)

3. *Gimme Gimme Gimme* and *Knowing Me, Knowing You*

4. 'Bohemian Rhapsody' and 'A Whiter Shade of Pale'

5. *Lulu* and *Salome* (spelt Salomé in the case of the Spanish Eurovision winner; the operas are adapted from plays by Frank Wedekind and Oscar Wilde respectively)

6. Sergio Agüero and Fernando Torres

7. Tony Benn and David Cameron (Benin and Cameroon)

8. Martin Clunes and Felicity Montagu

MOTION PICTURE MIXTURE

1. Katharine Hepburn (*Morning Glory*; *Rooster Cogburn*; *Suddenly, Last Summer*; *Bringing Up Baby*; *Love Among the Ruins*; *On Golden Pond*; *Adam's Rib*; *Little Women*; *Desk Set*)

2. Tom Hanks (*Toy Story* [and sequels]; *Angels and Demons*; *Sully*; *That Thing You Do!*; *Extremely Loud and Incredibly Close*; *Big*; *Cloud Atlas*)

[*]   Some have complained that composer Barrington Pheloung incorrectly spaced the two dashes that formed the 'M' so that it sounded more like 'T.T.O.R.S.E'. Sometimes the murderer's name would also be spelt out by the music. Ronnie Hazlehurst's theme for *Some Mothers Do 'Ave 'Em* also incorporates Morse code, spelling out the title of the series.

[**] Alexis Texas is an actress whose films include *Asses of Face Destruction 3*, *My Sister's Hot Friend 16* and *Buttwoman vs. Slutwoman*.

3. Meryl Streep (*It's Complicated*; *Still of the Night*; *Falling in Love*; *Out of Africa*; *Dancing at Lughnasa*; *Into the Woods*; *Dark Matter*; *Fantastic Mr Fox*; *Death Becomes Her*)

4. Kate Winslet (*Little Children*; *Steve Jobs*; *Eternal Sunshine of the Spotless Mind*; *Revolutionary Road*; *All the King's Men*; *Hideous Kinky*; *Holy Smoke!*; *Heavenly Creatures*; *Carnage*)

5. Nicole Kidman (*Cold Mountain*; *Dead Calm*; *Rabbit Hole*; *Before I Go to Sleep*; *My Life*; *Eyes Wide Shut*; *Happy Feet*; *Birthday Girl*)

6. Morgan Freeman (*Batman Begins*; *Kiss the Girls*; *Lucky Number Slevin*; *Robin Hood: Prince of Thieves*; *Driving Miss Daisy*; *Along Came a Spider*; *London Has Fallen*; *High Crimes*; *Street Smart*)

7. Julia Roberts (*Mystic Pizza*; *August: Osage County*; *Sleeping with the Enemy*; *Fireflies in the Garden*; *I Love Trouble*; *Eat Pray Love*; *My Best Friend's Wedding*; *Mother's Day*; *Mirror, Mirror*)

8. Alec Guinness (*Our Man in Havana*; *Father Brown*; *Great Expectations*; *Kind Hearts and Coronets*; *Star Wars*; *Barnacle Bill*; *Murder by Death*; *Hitler: The Last Ten Days*)

PART THREE: MAKING CONNECTIONS

SPOT THE LINK (NO. 1)

1. Silver (Argentina comes from the Latin *argentinus* ['of silver'], from *argentum* [silver]. Folk etymology sometimes traces Ireland to iron, but there is no evidence that this is true; the name is much more likely to derive from the goddess Ériu. It is also sometimes held that Cyprus was named after copper, but it is far more likely that the element was named after the island.)

2. Trotter

3. Honey

4. Sugar

5. Wormwood

6. Bucket (Kick the bucket/Ice Bucket Challenge)

7. Twit

8. They are surnames of Roald Dahl characters (Mrs Silver, the tortoise owner in *Esio Trot*; James Trotter from *James and the Giant Peach*; Miss Honey from *Matilda*; Henry Sugar from *The Wonderful Story of Henry Sugar*; Matilda Wormwood from *Matilda*; Charlie Bucket from *Charlie and the Chocolate Factory* and *Charlie and the Great Glass Elevator*; Mr and Mrs Twit from *The Twits*)

PICTURE CONNECTIONS

1. Examples of irony according to Alanis Morrisette's 'Ironic' ('a black fly in your Chardonnay'; 'a no-smoking sign on your cigarette break'; 'a traffic jam when you're already late'; 'rain on your wedding day')

2. Named after British prime ministers (Earl Grey tea; Gladstone bag; Wellington boots; Pittsburgh, after Pitt the Elder)

3. Surnames of comic-book heroes' alter egos (Bruce Wayne, Batman [Wayne Rooney was depicted in the picture]; Bruce Banner, the Incredible Hulk; Oliver Queen, Green Arrow; Clark Kent, Superman)

4. Types of mushroom (button, portobello, oyster, chestnut).

5. Nicknames of Margaret Thatcher (Iron Lady; Tina* [Tina Turner was depicted in the picture]; Attila the Hen; milk-snatcher)

6. US states with the first two letters removed (Diana; Io; Kansas; Egon [Schiele])

7. Names ending in powers of ten in French (Kim Jong-un; Otto Dix; 50 Cent; Cecil B. DeMille)

IT'S ANALOGY SEASON! (NO. 1)

1. Quarter note (British and American equivalents of musical notes)

2. The Jackson 5 (The song which is first in each pair is by a band which shares its name with a song by the band that is second in each pair: Jet and ABC)

3. 1/60 (Meanings of 'second' and 'minute' with the emphasis on the second syllable)

4. Henry VIII (Austen and Catwoman were among the roles of Anne Hathaway [in *Becoming Jane* and *The Dark Knight Rises* respectively], who is the namesake of Shakespeare's wife, while Solitaire and Dr Quinn were among the roles of Jane Seymour [in *Live and Let Die* and *Dr Quinn, Medicine Woman* respectively], who is the namesake of one of Henry VIII's wives)

---

*   This was an acronym for her catchphrase 'There is no alternative'.

5. An orange (they are shown to signify or portend a character's death)

6. Mexico City (the capital of Jersey is to the capital of New Jersey as the capital of Mexico is to the capital of New Mexico)

7. Adorable (what F and A stand for in the NATO phonetic alphabet and in the song 'A You're Adorable' [music by Sidney Lippman, lyrics by Fred Wise and Buddy Kaye])

8. Be (Songs beginning 'Let It...' and their authors)

EIGHT DEGREES OF KEVIN BACON

1. *Queer Eye for the Straight Guy*

2. Mustard

3. Nicki Minaj

4. Trevor McDonald

5. William Wordsworth

6. Squirrel

7. Beatrix Potter

8. Renée Zellweger

SPOT THE LINK (NO. 2)

1. May (James May's concealed message was: 'So you think it's really good, yeah? You should try making the bloody thing up. It's a real pain in the arse.')

2. Meat (Meat Puppets; Meat Loaf; *Meat is Murder*)

3. Cor

4. Kerr (Deborah and Judith)

5. Cava (a Catalan word originally meaning 'cellar' or 'cave')

6. Lout

7. Offal

8. They are all Irish counties with the final letter removed (Mayo; Meath; Cork; Kerry; Cavan; Louth; Offaly)

IT'S ANALOGY SEASON! (NO. 2)

1. Passover (Bookcase is to casebook as overpass is to...)

2. Iris Murdoch ('Maria' is to 'Maria Maria' as *The Sea* is to *The Sea, The Sea*)

3. The colours of the rainbow (they are mnemonic acronyms: Mrs Gren stands for Movement, Reproduction, Sensitivity, Growth, Respiration, Excretion, Nutrition; Roy G. Biv for Red, Orange, Yellow, Green, Blue, Indigo, Violet)

4. The telephone (Adam and Eve are to 'believe' [in Cockney rhyming slang] as dog and bone are to...)

5. The Netherlands (the first flag becomes the second when turned ninety degrees anti-clockwise)

6. Dastardly and Muttley (*Wacky Races* characters and their vehicles)

7. Ibis (the numbers in question appear to spell these words when typed into a calculator and turned upside down)

8. 2006 (*Time* Man/Person of the Year; 'You' won the 2006 award for contributing content to the Internet and 'controlling the Information Age'. Congratulations.)

WHAT DO THE FOLLOWING HAVE IN COMMON? (NO. 1)

1. They each share their surname with a member of the Smiths (Mickey/Andy Rourke; James/Mike Joyce; Neil/Steven Morrissey; Andrew/Johnny Marr)

2. They have no nose ('My dog's got no nose.' 'How does it smell?' 'Terrible!')*

3. All are nicknamed 'Duke' or 'the Duke'**

4. Can be followed by '-ettes' to make names of bands (Pip, Chord, Ron [Ron Burgundy, in the film *Anchorman: The Legend of Ron Burgundy*, and Ron Atkinson], Marvel)

5. They contain names of languages (Latin, Thai, Hindi and German)

6. They are locations or addresses of fictional bears (Rupert; Winnie-the-Pooh; Yogi Bear; and Paddington)

7. They are anagrams of countries (China, Algeria, Spain and Germany)

8. They were all succeeded in their jobs (king, poet laureate, butler to the Wayne family in Batman comics, England football manager) by a man named Alfred: the Great; Lord Tennyson; Pennyworth (Jarvis's son)***; Ramsey

---

*   Julia, a French mathematician known for his work on fractals, lost his nose in combat during the First World War.

**   Abdul Fakir (from the Four Tops) received the nickname from his mother; John Wayne received it in honour of Duke, an Airedale terrier from which he was inseparable as a child; David Dickinson explained in an interview that 'some wag' on the Internet bestowed it upon him because of his dress sense; and Duke Ellington received it, while still a child, for his debonair manners and dapper appearance.

*** Alfred's father's name was changed to Arthur in the TV series *Pennyworth*.

SPOT THE SIMILARITIES

A6 in Picture 1=A3 in Picture 2

E1 in Picture 1=F4 in Picture 2

E7 in Picture 1=C5 in Picture 2

G6 in Picture 1=E6 in Picture 2

A4 in Picture 1=A7 in Picture 2

D10 in Picture 1=C7 in Picture 2

E8 in Picture 1=B10 in Picture 2

F11 in Picture 1=G10 in Picture 2

IT'S ANALOGY SEASON! (NO. 3)

1. Desmond Tutu (degree results rhyming slang: Geoff [Hurst]/ Damien [Hirst] = first; Desmond = 2.ii)

2. A flat cap (keen bird is to bean curd as cat flap is to…)

3. Lily (replace the number in the word with its equivalent in Roman numerals: Mar**ten** is to Mar**x** as **lone**ly is to…)

4. David Brent (the name of the company and central character in the American and British versions of *The Office*)

5. 5 (*Scrabble* values)*

6. Fiver (from *Watership Down*); (Penny [Mordaunt] is to [Ezra] Pound as Fiver (slang for £5) is to Monkey (slang for £500))

7. Vangelis (remove the first and last letter: Cypress is to Ypres as Evangelist is to…)

8. Snap, Crackle and Pop

---

*   When I posed this to the pub, one team came up with the ingenious deduction that the numbers were double the combined number of strokes required to draw the letters they corresponded to, so I let them have their answer of 6.

WHAT DO THE FOLLOWING HAVE IN COMMON? (NO. 2)

1. They can be represented by the letter 'x'

2. They are versions of the *Fawlty Towers* sign seen during different episodes' opening sequence*

3. They are surnames of composers with surnames of other composers removed (Claudio Monteverdi, Jacques Offenbach and Arnold Schoenberg)

4. Each one is an example of itself (RAS syndrome stands for Redundant Acronym Syndrome syndrome [e.g. PIN number, where the 'N' already stands for 'number']; Stigler's law of eponymy states that no discovery is named after its original discoverer, with Stephen Stigler himself attributing it to Robert Merton; and sesquipedalianism [from the Latin for 'a foot and a half long'] is the practice of using long words)

5. They are films remade by the same director (George Sluizer; Cecil B. DeMille; Michael Haneke; Alfred Hitchcock)

6. They are musicians with the stage surname Dee (Mikkey Dee [Motörhead drummer]; Kool Moe Dee; Dave Dee; Kiki Dee)

7. They are all children of prime ministers (Violet Bonham Carter *née* Asquith; Carol Thatcher; William Pitt the Younger; Horace Walpole)

8. They come in packs

....
*   In the opening sequence of *The Psychiatrist*, the culprit behind the rearranging of the letters is finally revealed: it was the paper boy who appeared in the show's first episode, who is shown completing his handiwork before running away.

Time Flies Venn You're Having Fun

1. Philadelphia (left: spreadable cheeses; right: Tom Hanks films [*Apollo 13*; *The Terminal*; *Angels and Demons*])

2. Piper (left: surnames of fictional Peters* [Pan; Quince; Griffin]; right: words which can make new words when preceded by 'sand' [paper; castle; box])

3. Tom-tom or tan-tan (left: exact reduplicatives [Boo-Boo; Tintin; can-can]; right: percussion instruments)

4. Dover (left: towns in Kent [Sevenoaks; Sandwich; Deal]; right: words which begin with birds [*wren*ch; *crow*n; *goose*berries])

5. America (left: fictional captains [Planet; Haddock; Hook]; right: Simon and Garfunkel songs ['Bridge over Troubled Water'; 'Bookends'; 'The Boxer'])

6. Hooch (left: surnames of Hogwarts staff [Sprout; Lupin; Vector]; right: canine title characters of films [Skip; Marley; Beethoven])

7. Minim (left: palindromes [Otto from *The Simpsons*; kayak; bib]; right: musical notes)

....
*   Peter Piper is thought to have been based on the eighteenth-century French horticulturalist Pierre Poivre.

PART FOUR: POETIC JUSTICE

THE HIDDEN POEM

1. *Beauty and the Beast*

2. *Rhino What You Did Last Summer*

3. 'Good things come to those who wait' (from Guinness adverts)

4. *3 Feet High and Rising*

5. *The Wind in the Willows*[*]

6. *The Rime of the Ancient Mariner*

7. '...Baby One More Time'

8. William Blake ('And did those feet in ancient time')

WORDSEARCH POEM: BIRDS

Eider (Ing**redie**nts)

Ibis (impos**sibi**lity)

Rhea (neve**r hear**)

Warbler (quar**rel, brawl**)

Albatross (a**ssort a bla**ze)

Lory (g**lory**)

Bittern (or tern) (**bitter, n**auseous)

Egret (r**egret**)

Lark (emotiona**l ark**)

Crane (betwe**en arc**haic)

Ostrich (**lost rich**es)

....
[*]   Rat and Mole are the ones who encounter Pan, who then wipes their memories of
        the experience.

Swan (venomou**s wan**derers)

Duck (dar**k cud**gelling)

Myna (**any m**ite)

Petrel (a**lert, ep**hemeral)

Linnet (ephemera**l in net**her)

Heron (net**her on**eness)

Erne (tend**erne**ss)

Anagram Poem: Fictional Birds

Woody Woodpecker

Mother Goose

Scrooge McDuck

Captain Flint (Long John Silver's parrot)

Howard the Duck

The Little Red Hen

Jonathan Livingston Seagull

Moses the raven (from *Animal Farm*)

Jemima Puddle-Duck

Wordsearch Poem: Capitals

Harare (wit**h a rare**) (Zimbabwe)

Valletta (th**at tell a v**ivid) (Malta)

Berlin (Decem**ber lin**gers) (Germany)

Lima (dre**amil**y) (Peru)

Athens (bre**ath ens**wathed) (Greece)

Hanoi (Mot**ion./A h**ibernating) (Vietnam)

Bern (hi**bern**ating) (Switzerland)

Lomé (d**emol**ishing) (Togo)

Astana (oce**an…/A Tsa**r) (Kazakhstan)

Rome (**remor**se) (Italy)

Oslo (**No slo**uching) (Norway)

Maseru (meas**ures!/A m**ad) (Lesotho)

Doha (libi**do ha**s) (Qatar)

Helsinki (satc**hel/Sinki**ng) (Finland)

Kingston (sin**king ston**es) (Jamaica)

Paris (u**p, arise**) (France)

Minsk (Brah**min sk**ies) (Belarus)

Malé (**male**dict) (Maldives)

THE CLERIHEWS OF E. C. BENTLEY

1. Sir Humphry Davy

2. Henry the First

3. Sir Christopher Wren

4. Mr Hilaire Belloc*

5. Cimabue

6. John Keats**

7. Ramsay MacDonald

8. John Stuart Mill

....

*   Belloc published travel writing, poetry for children, and works on politics and economics.

**   The line 'full of the true, the blushful Hippocrene' is from 'Ode to a Nightingale'. Hippocrene, in Greek mythology, is a spring whose water produces poetic inspiration when drunk.

WORDSEARCH POEM: CHEESE

Port Salut (Taran**tula's troph**y)

Emmental (po**em/Mental**)

Cheshire (lee**ches, hire**lings)

Limburger (**Climb, urge, r**ansack)

Edam (un**made**)

Stilton (brain**s,/'Til ton**gues)

Cheddar (a**ched – dar**e)

Wensleydale (fearsom**e Lady El's new**)

Feta (h**ateful**)

Boursin (cur**b our sin**ful)

Brie (so**brie**ty)

Yarg (stin**gray**)

Ricotta (ap**ricot ta**rt)

Comté (swe**et,/Moc**k)

Derby (asun**der by**)

ANAGRAM POEM: FICTIONAL EDUCATION

St Trinian's

Hogwarts (from *Harry Potter*)

Dotheboys Hall (from *Nicholas Nickleby* by Charles Dickens)

Malory Towers

Grange Hill

Sunnydale High (from *Buffy the Vampire Slayer*)

Springfield Elementary (from *The Simpsons*)

Starfleet Academy (from *Star Trek*)

Porterhouse College (from *Porterhouse Blue* by Tom Sharpe)

THE RHYMESTER'S FURY

1. Caraway and faraway
2. Suggest and smuggest
3. Lavish and knavish*
4. Ague and plague
5. Assist and bassist
6. Discount and viscount
7. Headdress and readdress
8. Dalliance and alliance

WORDSEARCH POEM: BONES

Tarsus (ver**sus Rat**s)

Ulna (m**an, Lu**scious)

Mandible (com**mand! I ble**ed)

Patella (m**allet, a p**ain)

Radius (jiu-jit**su, I dar**e)

Carpals (**Slap rac**coons)

Femur (d**rum ef**fects)

Pubis (coy**pu, bis**ect)

....

*   'O Lord our God arise,
      Scatter his enemies
      And make them fall;
      Confound their politics,
      Frustrate their knavish tricks,
      On Thee our hopes we fix,
      God save us all!'

Sacrum (a**s a crum**pet)

Phalanx (nym**phal anx**ieties)

Vertebrae (f**ear! Be Trev**or)

Maxilla (**max, ill a**t)

Sternum (Ma**ster num**berless)

Stapes (wildebee**st, apes**)

Malleus (Pur**sue llam**as)

Tibia (Mumb**ai, bit**e)

COMPLETE THE LIMERICKS

1. Tokyo Tower*

2. Jane Eyre

3. A.C. (Ashley Cole, who wore the number three shirt for most of his career, and Alan Carr, host of *Alan Carr: Chatty Man*)

4. Tarantella (which folk etymology links to a dancing epidemic caused by tarantula bites, though it's more likely that the names of both the dance and the spider are derived from the city of Taranto, in the Apulia region of Italy)

5. Grace Kelly

6. Mata Hari**

7. 'Fight My Lyre'

8. Robert Peel

....

*   The shade of red used on the Tokyo Tower is known as 'international orange'. The tower had to be painted white and international orange to comply with air safety regulations.

**   The limerick alludes to how Mata Hari (born Margaretha Zelle), a Dutch dancer and courtesan, was accused by French authorities during the First World War of being a German spy and subsequently executed.

WORDSEARCH POEM: MYTHICAL CREATURES

Centaur (des**cent Aur**ally)

Wyvern (de**wy vern**acular)

Sasquatch (A**s a squat ch**ild)

Troll (counci**llor t**akes)

Cerberus (Un**sure Brec**ht)

Gnome (L**emon g**lorifies)

Manticore (ro**mantic or e**ven)

Hydra (foolh**ardy. H**e's)

Banshee (tur**ban, shee**pish)

Werewolf (wall**flower. Ew**er)

Satyr (fie**ry tas**te)

Fairy (S**yria, F**allujah)

Ogress (or ogre) (retr**ogress**ive)

Goblin (**go blin**d...)

Golem (**go Lem**on.")

Gremlin ("One-**nil!", merg**ing)

MORE ELOQUENCE THAN YOU COULD SHAKE A SPEAR AT

1. To thine own self be true (Will Self)

2. Out, damned spot

3. Parting is such sweet sorrow

4. Uneasy lies the head that wears a crown

5. What light through yonder window breaks?

6. Salad days

7. There is a tide in the affairs of men

COMPLETE THE LIMERICKS (ANOTHER WAY)

1. etchers/Chester/retches
2. Nepal/panel/plane
3. Dorset/stored/sorted
4. praised/despair/aspired
5. residents/tiredness/dissenter
6. salesmen/lameness/nameless
7. teardrop/*Predator*/parroted
8. listen/Silent/tinsel

WORDSEARCH POEM: CARS

Mercedes (super**sede crem**atoria)

Alfa Romeo (a p**oem (or a fla**me?))

Volvo (Pav**lov lov**e)

Citroën (a bo**ne/Or tic**kle)

Tesla (**falset**to)

Cadillac (**call,/'I'd ac**he)

Fiat (Vi**ta, if**)

Ford (hy**drof**luoric)

Seat (nau**seat**ing)

Opel (need**lepo**int)

Porsche (stu**pors,/Che**w)

Honda (crunc**h on da**inty)

Subaru (dishono**ur, abus**e)

Mini (di**mini**sh)

Audi (indiv**idua**l)

Daewoo (t**o owe a d**og)

Anagram Poem: Women Who Changed the World

Marie Stopes

Dusty Springfield

Emmeline Pankhurst

Vivienne Westwood

Sybil Thorndike

Jacqueline du Pré

Stella Rimington

Elizabeth David

Caroline Lucas

PART FIVE: WORDPLAY

HOLY MACKEREL!

1. Tin

2. Indigo

3. Down

4. Job

5. Just visiting

6. *Gigi** and *Wings***

7. Djibouti and Togo

8. Ohio

   (The London Underground station mentioned in the footnote is St John's Wood)

2 BECOME 1 (NO. 1)

1. Lava tory/lavatory

2. Imp lore/implore

3. Capri corn/Capricorn

4. Lace ration/laceration

5. Roman tic/romantic

6. Just ice/justice

7. Late rally/laterally

8. Pronoun cement/pronouncement

---

*   Lyricist Alan Jay Lerner, composer Frederick Loewe and set, production and costume designer Cecil Beaton, who were all involved in *Gigi,* had previously been involved in the Broadway version of *My Fair Lady* (the film of which would not come out until 1964).

**   As of 2023 these are the only Best Picture winners not to contain any letters of the word 'mackerel'.

FILL IN THE BLANKS

1. fathoming/fat homing

2. carpentry/carp entry

3. stagnancy/stag Nancy

4. them iller), stale/*The Miller's Tale*

5. unclean) drew/uncle Andrew

6. Wimbledon/Wim* bled on

7. Klee next issue's/Kleenex tissues

8. Dre's sage/dressage**

ADD THE ANIMAL

1. Complied/Compli**cat**ed

2. Agonise/**Ant**agonise

3. Brie/Brie**fly**

4. Tumbled/Tumbl**ewe**ed

5. Lies/**Lotter**ies

6. Begged/B**owl**egged

7. Tom/To**pony**m

8. Part/Par**ape**t or **Ram**part

ANAGRAMS PLUS ONE (No. 1)

1. Glen (*Glengarry Glen Ross* and *Monarch of the Glen*)

2. Angel***

3. Ang Lee****

---

*   Wim Wenders, that is.

**   Dr. Dre's sage advice is taken from 'Let Me Ride'.

***   The TV series *Angel* is a spin-off from *Buffy the Vampire Slayer*.

**** The illustration depicts John Wayne saying, 'Slap some bacon on a biscuit and let's go! We're burnin' daylight!' This is a line from *The Cowboys*. I am informed that the Chinese translation is quite loose.

4. Al Green

5. Generals (General Zod is an enemy of Superman; General Grievous appears in *Star Wars: Clone Wars* and *Revenge of the Sith*; and General Yen is from *The Bitter Tea of General Yen*, a Grace Zaring Stone novel made into a Frank Capra film)

6. Lestrange

7. *Silent Rage*

8. Nigel Slater

PALINDROME (NO. 1)

1. Tennessee

2. Molasses

3. Oman

4. Elena (Gilbert; Baltacha; Ceaușescu, born Lenuța Petrescu)

5. Moses

6. Salome

7. Essen

8. Net

IT ALL ADDS UP: TELEVISION

1. *Brookside* (Backside – axe + rooks)

2. *Blockbusters* (Boilers – oil + lock bust)

3. *Miranda* (Millennia – Lenny [from *The Simpsons*] + rand)

4. *Grey's Anatomy* (Goatee – oat + raisin atom)

5. *In Sickness and in Health* (Inn, sixteenth – [Jock] Stein + Nissan [logo with letters removed] din Hell)

6. *Jackanory* (Jam artery – martyr + Knorr [stock cubes, with logo removed])

7. *Loose Women* (Loo, cabin – cab + swim)

Anagrams: Personal Ads

Silver Linings Playbook

When Harry Met Sally

The Philadelphia Story

Pretty in Pink

The Wedding Singer

The Apartment

My Best Friend's Wedding

Forgetting Sarah Marshall

There's Something About Mary

Crawl Inside My Idiom Attic

1. The bush (beat around or about the bush/a bird in the hand is worth two in the bush)

2. Bee (busy as a bee/bee's knees)

3. Cheese (big cheese/as different as chalk and cheese)

4. Dutch (treat/uncle/courage)

5. Mustard (keen as mustard/cut the mustard)

6. Scratch (start from scratch/up to scratch)

7. Board (above board/across the board)

8. Cat (curiosity killed the cat/cat got your tongue)

Alphabetical Antics (No. 1)

1. Jock

2. Mr. T

3. Few ('Never in the field of human conflict was so much owed by so many to so few'*/'We few, we happy few, we band of brothers')

4. PhD (the Klitschko brothers in sports science; May in astrophysics)

5. V

6. Lynx

7. Quiz**

8. Bags

Gogglebox Jigsaw

1. Ill

2. W

3. To

4. *How*

5. Iona

6. Beam

7. Ire

8. Ants; *Who Wants to be a Millionaire?* (if the order of the answers is changed to 2, 4, Ants, 3, 6, 1, 5, 7)

....

*   Reportedly, Churchill had originally intended to say, 'Never in the history of mankind has so much been owed by so many to so few' in his speech, until it was pointed out that this would include Jesus and his disciples.

**   Several words (such as 'zizz' or 'jazz') would outscore 'quiz' if there were more than one *z* in a standard *Scrabble* set.

WORDS OF CHARACTER

1. Mini-Me

2. Pamphlet (the character was Pamphilus, from the Greek *pamphilos*)

3. Poindexter

4. Ignoramus*

5. Brainiac

6. Goody two-shoes

7. Paparazzo

8. Lothario

PALINDROME (NO. 2)

1. Iona (becoming 'Ionian' with the addition of extra letters)

2. Hero

3. *Gladiator***

4. Toto

5. Trot

6. Aid (Christian Aid/Hearing aid/Band Aid)

7. Al Gore

8. Hanoi (Ho Chi Minh being the president)

....

*   The play lasted six hours and was greatly enjoyed by James I, who attended its first performance.

**   'It was a stone cold masterpiece,' remarked Cave, who had been approached by Russell Crowe to pen the sequel. 'I enjoyed writing it very much because I knew on every level that it was never going to get made'.

Build Your Own Wordsearch

1. Meathead

2. Charisma

3. Limerick

4. Punk rock

5. Postmark

6. Tribally (Lily Bart being the character)

7. Benzylic

8. Lacrosse

Hidden names: Meath; Laois; Clare; Leitrim; Cork; Mayo (Irish counties, along with Limerick)

Alphabetical Antics (No. 2)

1. Flax

2. Quick

3. R

4. *Spy*

5. DJ (*Last Night a DJ Saved my Life*)

6. Boz (Boz Scaggs being the musician)

7. *GMTV*

8. When ('a Man Loves a Woman'/'I'm Sixty-Four')

2 BECOME 1 (NO. 2)

1. Incan descent/incandescent
2. Mole station/molestation
3. Disco lour/discolour
4. Mist rust/mistrust
5. Heat hen/heathen
6. Overt Ure/overture (A reference to Midge Ure)
7. Fig urine/figurine
8. Hippo crates/Hippocrates

WORDS WITH WOMEN

1. Leg and Le**ering**
2. Bar and B**esme**ar
3. Delete and De**cath**lete
4. Cling and Cl**amber**ing
5. Sot and So**lois**t
6. Pun and Pu**rita**n
7. Cry and **Mimi**cry
8. Faded and Fa**thea**ded

THE END IS THE BEGINNING IS THE END

1. Djibouti

2. Lennon (the son of Liam)

3. James

4. Help yourself

5. Frank (*300* being the Frank Miller-inspired film)

6. Evelyn Waugh

7. Melville*

8. Francis Bacon

PALINDROME (NO. 3)

1. Niagara

2. Cyrano de Bergerac

3. Soho**

4. Scare

5. Grebe

6. Donary

7. Car

8. Again

---

*   Richard Hall is better known as Moby.
**   New York's SoHo is an abbreviation of 'South of Houston Street' (as well as being a
       reference to its London counterpart).

Anagrams Plus One (No. 2)

1. Air
2. Iran*
3. Nairn
4. Narnia
5. *Rain Man*
6. Mandarin
7. Dan Marino
8. Prima donna

Backwards Cinema

1. *The Big Peels***
2. *The Twilight Agas*
3. *Rail Liar*
4. *Kramer vs. Remark* (or *Remark vs. Kramer*)
5. *How the West Was Now*
6. *You've Got Liam*
7. *The Longest Dray*
8. *Reknit Tailor Soldier Spy*

Hidden Lands

1. Chile (Gnoc**chi/Le**icester)
2. Mongolia (Solo**mon/Golia**th)
3. Brunei (Irn-**Bru/Nei**l Young)

....
*   At the time of writing, Iran is the only country where it is legal to sell one's kidneys.
**   *The Big Sleep* was advertised with the tagline 'The Violence-Screen's All-Time Rocker-Shocker!'

4. Eritrea (Berib**eri/Trea**son)

5. Burundi (Excali**bur/Undi**sputed)

6. Belarus ('Rebel Re**bel'/*A Rus*h** of Blood to the Head)

7. Yemen (Pope**ye*/Men**tor)

8. Slovenia ('All You Need I**s Love'/*Nia*gara**)

REBUS CROSSWORD

Part One:

1. Echolocate (Ecole oak eight)

2. Pilfer (Pill fur)

3. Pillowcase (Pill oak ace)

4. Perfumery (Purr phew Marie)

5. Perforate (Purr fur eight)

6. *Fawlty Towers* (Fall teat hours)

7. Marine outfall (Marie nowt fall)

8. Tea towel (Teat owl)

Part Two:

1e (Eight)

2h (Teat)

3a (Pill)

4g (Fall)

5b (Oak)

6c (Purr)

7d (Fur)

8f (Marie)

....

*   Alma, Arkansas, which also claims to be the 'spinach capital of the world', has its own
    statue of Popeye.

PART SIX: LET'S GO EXPLORING*

DISCO ISLAND DES

1. The Hustle (*Hustle* being the series)

2. Reveries and rediscoveries

3. Funkytown (formed from *Fun*afuti, *Kyo*to and Free*town*; the song is by Lipps Inc)

4. Chic (formed from 'Psychic' with 'Psy' removed)

5. Diana Ross

6. 'Rock the Oat' ('Rock the Boat' being the original title)

7. A YMCA

8. H (Donna Summer being the Queen of Disco)**

HENRIETTA SNEEP, SPEECH THERAPIST

1. *Rock of Ages*

2. With a little help from my friends, she's leaving home when I'm sixty-four

3. B as P ('Batter' as 'patter' and 'Big Ben' as 'pig pen')

4. *Monty Python's Life of Brian* ('He's not the Messiah, he's a very naughty boy!')

5. Ite (Fin[ite]/Reign[ite])

6. Highfaluting (Haifa looting)

7. The Lord's Prayer ('Give us this day our daily bread')

8. Grant; Pierce; Harrison; Ford***

---

* This part takes its name from the final line of dialogue of Bill Watterson's *Calvin and Hobbes*.

** Sylvester was also known as the Queen of Disco.

*** George Hamilton-Gordon and Robert Gascoyne-Cecil are better known as the Earl of Aberdeen and the Marquess of Salisbury respectively. The phrase 'Bob's your uncle' is thought to derive from Lord Salisbury's appointment of his nephew, future prime minister Arthur Balfour, as Chief Secretary for Ireland.

Advent Calendar of Doom

1. 23

2. 12 (*Twelve Monkeys*, *Ocean's Twelve*, *12 Years a Slave*)

3. 7 (*Seven*, *Seven Years in Tibet*, *Sinbad: Legend of the Seven Seas*)

4. 10

5. 17

6. 15 ('9 to 5'/'Three Little Birds')

7. 3 (Ether)

8. 16

Chemical Element Blind Date

1. Aluminium (a reference to it losing its right 'i' in US English, as well to the Paul Simon song 'You Can Call Me Al' [Al being its chemical symbol])

2. Carbon (Referring to carbon dating and diamond being an allotrope of carbon)

3. Iron (ruling with a rod of iron/pumping iron)

4. Magnesium (atomic number 12, symbol Mg)

5. Xenon* (X symbolising a kiss, and xenon can be used in anaesthetics)

6. Cadmium (symbol: Cd)

7. Tin (referring to a tin ear and 'abstinence' becoming 'absence' without it)

8. Gold (*ABBA Gold*/gold digger)

---

* In 1962 Neil Bartlett synthesised xenon hexafluoroplatinate, thereby disproving the widely held belief that noble gases were inert.

RIDDLES OF THE SPHINX

1. Squash

2. Fairness (fins/Ares)

3. Reith (John Reith, the BBC's founder and its first director general)

4. Blue (the riddle refers to the beard colour by which each is known: Wizard Whitebeard; Blackbeard; *Yellowbeard*; Bluebeard)

5. Tackle ('elk' and 'cat' backwards)

6. Rodin (Remove 'R' to form 'Odin', after whom Wednesday is named, then remove 'O' to get 'din')

7. *Martin Chuzzlewit* and *Bleak House*

8. A coat hanger (c + oath + anger)

GROUNDHOG DAY

1. It is unclimbed, and not allowed to be climbed (thus contradicting the line 'There ain't no hill or mountain we can't climb'; in 1994 a law was passed forbidding the climbing of mountains higher than 6000 metres, and in 2003 mountaineering was banned altogether. Gangkhar Puensum is the world's highest unclimbed peak.)

2. Glee (both Ryersons are portrayed by Stephen Tobolowsky)

3. 60

4. Lilliput (Lemuel Gulliver, in *Gulliver's Travels*)

5. Baby

6. Decisiveness (SSE stands for South-Southeast, thus the opposite of North by Northwest, Nevis is a reference to Ben Nevis and 'iced' means 'frozen'; SSE Nevis iced spelt backwards is decisiveness.)

7. Palindrome (02/02/2020)

8. Charles I (when awaiting execution)

1. Beavis and Butt-Head

2. Hound Dog Gray (Dorian Gray)

3. Rectangle ('Wreck tangle')

4. Pal in Rome

5. *Brokeback Mountain*

6. All's well (if you remove each of these letters from each of the sounds in turn, it transforms each sound into a palindrome.)

7. They are weather forecasters

8. Victoria (capital of the Seychelles)

1. Harry Nilsson ('Gotta Get Up')

2. Woodchuck

3. Portugal (Mire = swampy bog; Redo = start again; Sore = source of pain; Fado = music from Portugal. Each word is made up of two notes; when the two notes of the first in each pair are both shifted one note lower, they spell out the second in each pair.)

4. 'Correct Ang Lee film' (Phil was unable to use the string of letters 'rectangle'.)

5. 42 (A hard yellow fruit is a quince, which is spelt identically to the Spanish for 'fifteen'; a synonym for 'collar' is 'seize', which is spelt identically to the French for 'sixteen'; and a helper of Santa Claus is an elf, which is spelt identically to the German for 'eleven'.)

6. The Heimlich manoeuvre (or abdominal thrusts)

7. Public liability (an anagram of CII Lilliput Baby)

8. St John's (capital of Antigua and Barbuda)

The Murder Mystery

Round 1:

1. Nigeria (North, 7)

2. Ely (East, 3)

3. Sunderland (South, 10)

4. Waldorf (West, 7)

5. Nirvana (North, 7)

6. Washington (West, 10)

7. Snickers (the undergarment being knickers) (South, 8)

8. *Emma* (East, 4)

Round 2:

1a. Prince (the film being *Purple Rain*)

1b. Crippen (P)

2a. Oregon

2b. Oregano (A)

3a. (The) Pantheon

3b. (The) Parthenon (R)

4a. Hilton (James and Paris)

4b. Lothian (A)

5a. Midstream

5b. Mastermind (N)

6a. Marina (Abramović and Lewycka)

6b. Romania (O)

7a. Camera*

*   The play was by John Van Druten.

7b. America (Ferrera) (I)

8a. Chester (A. Arthur)

8b. Teachers (A)

Round 3:

1. Tarzan (in the language of the Mangani, the fictional species of great apes among whom Tarzan grows up)

2. Adam Lallana

3. Canada

4. Casablanca

5. Batman (in the film *The Dark Knight*)

6. Caravan

7. Franz Kafka

8. *Mars Attacks!*

Rebus: Weapons

1. Rapier (Ray; pier)

2. Boomerang (boo; meringue)

3. Homing missile (hoe; Ming [the Merciless, from *Flash Gordon*]; miss; isle)

4. Light rifle (lie; trifle)

5. Napalm (neigh; palm)

6. Pepper spray (Pep [Guardiola]; purse; pray)

7. Halberd (HAL [from *2001: A Space Odyssey*]; bird)

8. Mousetrap (Mao; strap)

Round 4:

1. C5

2. E11 (EXI: existing, exigent, sexily, coexist)

3. K12 (K12)

4. J9 (J[a]nine)

5. J6 ('Back to Basics', title of albums and Tory campaign)

6. L5 (Elf Ive)

7. J4 (the novel being *Three Men in a Boat [To Say Nothing of the Dog]*)

8. C3(PO)

9. G5 (Fi [Glover], jive!)

10. H8 (height)

11. J3 (the three states are Pennsylvania, Mississippi and New Hampshire)

12. I1

13. B1 (Bo[vi]ne)

14. A10

15. D12

16. B9 (Benin [the first two being Algeria and Angola] – B nine)

AND FINALLY...

Room: Study

Motive: Paranoia

Weapon: Napalm (contains 'a' as its only vowel)

Murderer: Claudiella Truckleshaw

The revelation:

After Sir Harbledon had stormed out, he retreated to his study to write an essay on the behaviour of fish. There he was discovered by Claudiella, who was on her way to the owlery to visit an austere-looking owl whom she had long considered the closest thing she had to a soulmate. As it happened, at the moment she passed her father he was illustrating his essay with a sketch of a whitemargin unicornfish, which in a fit of paranoia she took to be an unflattering caricature of herself. She burned him to death with napalm, which she had taken to carrying around with her after an autocorrect-based error left her inadvertently ordering Dolores to prepare napalm jelly instead of elderflower jelly. She dragged the body through the manor, hoping to hide it in the garden hedge before dropping the body and diving into the kitchen at the sound of approaching footsteps.

TIE BREAKERS

1. 7392

2. 557*

3. 1917 (in a letter to Winston Churchill from Lord Fisher)

4. 171

5. 3308 (Pongo has 72 spots, Perdita has 68 and the puppies have 32 each)

6. £194400

7. 989

8. 324 (the game has 6 suspects, 6 weapons and 9 rooms)

---

*   A man in the pub was very insistent that, in actual fact, *no one* speaks Cornish anymore and that the 557 people who had claimed to speak it had done so out of either a sense of Cornish national pride or the desire to make mischief.

ACKNOWLEDGEMENTS

A thousand thanks to Steve Kupfer, who pored over the text and made astoundingly astute remarks, and who is very much missed. Also thanks to Luke Ingram, who is my agent, to everyone at Oneworld, who are absolutely wonderful to work with, and to Gesche Ipsen, without whom this book would simply be a hazy throng of thoughts in my head, accompanied by a slight sense of frustration that I could not share them with as many people as I would wish. Thanks also to Arnet Addis, who gave me the idea for the 'What's the Difference?' and 'Time Flies Venn You're Having Fun' rounds, to David Shallcross, who performed the unenviable task of translating 'Slap some bacon on a biscuit and let's go! We're burnin' daylight!' into Chinese, and to Owen Holland, who was the first to describe my quizzes as 'cryptic pub quizzes'.

I'm deeply grateful for the existence of www.greenehouse.com/a/ jangler-enigma, a database maintained by Andrew Greene detailing examples of words manipulated in various ways to form other words, which was an invaluable resource in compiling word puzzles.

Thanks to everyone who has come to, and continues to come to, my quiz at The Mill – you bring a great deal of fulfilment to me. And thanks to the staff at The Mill for giving me the chance to realise my quizzing dreams.

Frank Paul has gathered the best of hundreds of rounds of pub quizzes into this book. Alongside the questions – and often forming part of the questions – are his drawings, which are as intricate as the puzzles. He is an Only Connect champion. He lives in Cambridge with his wife and their three children.

NOTES

NOTES

NOTES

NOTES

NOTES

NOTES

NOTES

NOTES

NOTES